# ARCHAEOLOGY
## A BRIEF INTRODUCTION

### THIRD EDITION

## BRIAN M. FAGAN

UNIVERSITY OF CALIFORNIA, SANTA BARBARA

SCOTT, FORESMAN AND COMPANY
GLENVIEW, ILLINOIS   BOSTON   LONDON

## TO

Lucia, Karen, and other friends at Whittier College who gave me the idea for this book.

And, as usual, to the formidable felines, Meat Loaf and Phaedra, who were as subversive as ever. They did everything they could to prevent me from revising the manuscript by stepping on it with muddy paws. As you can see, they failed!

Library of Congress Cataloging-in-Publication Data

Fagan, Brian M.
  Archaeology: a brief introduction.

  Bibliography: p.209
  Includes index.
  1. Archaeology.   I. Title.
CC165.F28   1987        930.1        87-2831
ISBN 0-673-39719-X (pbk.)

2   3   4   5   6   7   8   9   10–KPF–93   92   91   90   89   88

Printed in the United States of America

Produced by R. David Newcomer Associates

Credits for illustrations appear on pages 221–222.

# TO THE
# READER

Archaeology always seems an exciting and romantic subject, especially when you read about the magnificent tomb of
the golden pharaoh Tutankhamun or the imposing Maya temples of the Yucatan. Most archaeological sites are less spectacular and are excavated on a far smaller scale. But that does
not make them any less fascinating for archaeologist and non-
archaeologist alike. This book is designed to give you some
idea of how archaeologists go about studying human behavior of the past. We cover the basic concepts and methods of
archaeological research—excavation, survey, analysis of artifacts and food remains, and such topics as dating and the
dimensions of time and space. *Archaeology: A Brief Introduction*
ends with a look at career prospects in archaeology and at
ways in which individuals—like you—can help save the past
for future generations. References for more detailed readings
are given at the end of the book.

I hope that this short text will give you new insights into
the fascinating world of the past. Good luck with your ad-
ventures in archaeology!

# TO THE
# INSTRUCTOR

This book is designed as a brief introduction to the fundamental principles of method and theory in archaeology. We begin with the goals of archaeology, go on to consider the basic concepts of culture, time, and space, and discuss the finding and excavation of archaeological sites. The last four chapters summarize some of the ways in which archaeologists order and study their finds. Throughout the book, I emphasize the ethics behind archaeology. We end with the vital question of how nonarchaeologists should relate to the finite resources that form the archaeological record. In my experience this subject is often neglected in introductory anthropology courses.

Our assumption is that this small book will act as supplementary reading for a general course on anthropology, and that your students will spend two or three weeks on the subject matter. Every attempt has been made to keep technical jargon to a minimum. Inevitably, a book of this length and scope glosses over many complex problems or smoldering controversies. I have proceeded on the assumption that a positive overstatement is better than a complex piece of inconclusive reasoning, at this stage in learning. Errors of overstatement can always be corrected in class or at a more advanced stage.

If there is a theme to *Archaeology*, it is that the patterning of archaeological artifacts we find in the ground can give us valuable insights into human behavior in the past. In pursuing this theme, I have attempted to focus on the basic concepts of archaeology. I leave you to impose your own theoretical viewpoints on the various chapters that follow. My assumption is, too, that you will fill in such additional details as you feel your students need. For this reason, I have drawn again and again on a few well-known sites from New and

Old World archaeology, such as Olduvai Gorge and Teoti-huacán, rather than distracting the reader with a multitude of site names. At the suggestion of several users, I have added brief descriptions of these major sites in a special "Site Information" section at the back of the book.

Space limitations prevent us from adding bibliographic references throughout the text. A short guide to further reading appears at the back of the book.

The third edition of *Archaeology* includes suggestions made by dozens of instructors and students. Many of the latter took the trouble to write to me even while they were using the book, making their comments even more useful and immediate. I am deeply grateful for their input, and hope that my changes reflect their interests. *Archaeology* has stood the test of time well, and so the changes we have made this time around are relatively small. The book has been updated throughout. The sections on analogy, typology, and subsistence have been rewritten, and Cultural Resource Management research integrated more closely into the body of the text. Some minor errors have been corrected; sites and chronologies have been updated. We have changed some illustrations and brought the references up to date. The general principles, though, have not changed. They provide the foundation for all the multifarious research projects that archaeologists carry out, as near home as California, and as far away as New Zealand.

I am grateful to all those who criticized the second edition, sent me information, or read portions of the revised manuscript. My grateful thanks to Thomas Volman of Cornell University, Katherine Spielmann of the University of Iowa, and Peter Ramsden of McMaster University, who reviewed *Archaeology* before revision. Any suggestions for improving future editions of this book would be greatly appreciated.

# CONTENTS

# 1

# ARCHAEOLOGY AS ANTHROPOLOGY

Archaeology is the special concern of a certain type of anthropologist.

JAMES DEETZ, 1967

## ARCHAEOLOGY

"Archaeology is the science of Rubbish," wrote British archaeologist Stuart Piggott some years ago. His definition conjures up a pleasing image of archaeologists delving deeply into innumerable ancient rubbish heaps. Piggott is partly right. Many archaeologists do spend their time digging up long-abandoned rubbish, and sometimes even modern trash. But the popular image of an archaeologist is somewhat more glamorous—the archaeologist as treasure hunter. Everyone has seen cartoons of the bearded, bespectacled archaeologist digging in the foundations of a mighty pyramid.

Then, too, our complex world is full of "unexplained" mysteries and hidden surprises. Many people believe that the archaeologist lives in the mysterious regions of our world, with grinning skeletons, "missing links," and long-lost civilizations. Enterprising authors and movie producers take us on fantasy rides into these strange territories of their specially selected archaeologists. From the comfort of our armchairs, via television, we can search for lost continents, reconstruct Noah's Ark, and trace the landing patterns of extraterrestrial astronauts' spaceships. Such searches for "lost mysteries" are not only fantasy fun but big business as well. Millions of dollars have been made from this type of archaeology,

2

FIGURE 1.1 The pyramids of Giza in Egypt. "The romance of archaeology has taken people all over the world in search of the past."

though, unfortunately, this world bears little resemblance to reality.

The romance of archaeology has taken people all over the world in search of the past. Thousands of tourists visit the pyramids of *Giza*[1] in Egypt every year (Figure 1.1). The Mexican government spent millions of pesos restoring the ancient city of *Teotihuacán* in the Valley of Mexico to promote tourism. Most popular package tours abroad now include visits to an archaeological site or two (Figure 1.2). Many sites, like *Stonehenge* in England and *Lascaux* in France, are in danger of permanent damage from the sheer volume of tourists who visit them. As a result, you can no longer wander among the uprights at Stonehenge. The French government has built a magnificent replica of the Lascaux cave paintings for tourists to enjoy, but the original is closed to all but scientists. Any thinking person who visits an archaeological site faces the

[1]Italicized site names are described in the "Site Information" section at the back of the book.

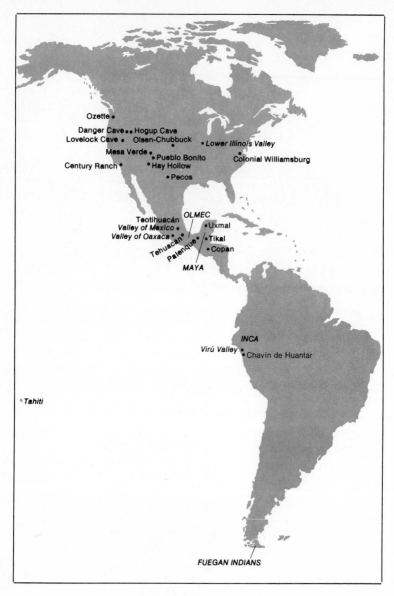

FIGURE 1.2 The archaeological sites mentioned in this text. Obvious geographic place names are omitted.

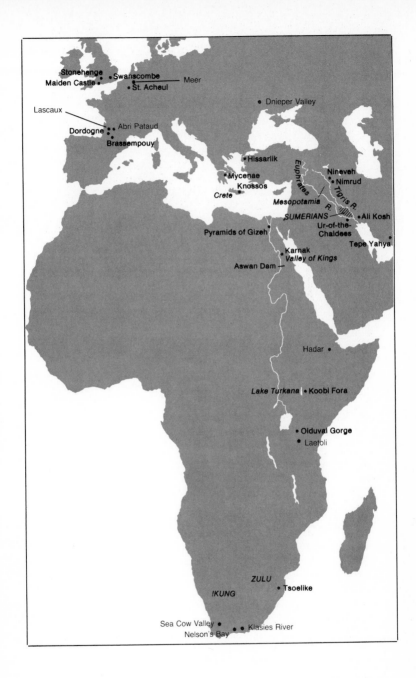

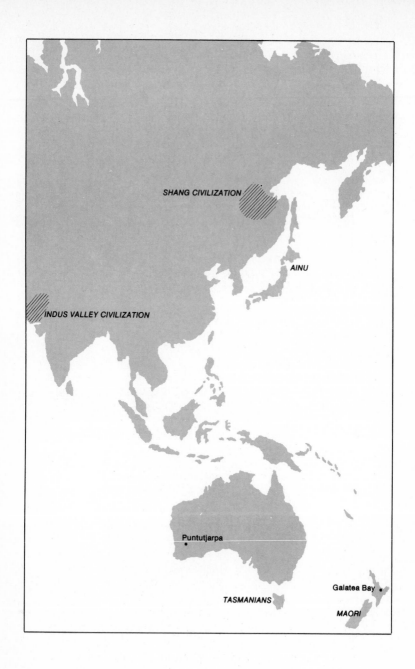

SHANG CIVILIZATION

AINU

INDUS VALLEY CIVILIZATION

Puntutjarpa

Galatea Bay

TASMANIANS

MAORI

reality of the past, a vista of human experience that stretches far back into remote time. How, visitors may wonder, do archaeologists know how old a site is, and what do the finds made in their digs mean? It all seems very complicated to dig for the past. And the unchanging, incredibly ancient structures that surround one add to one's sense of romance and awe.

Most such archaeological sites now boast a museum. Eagerly, the tourist leans over the display cases and admires the glittering gold of a fine necklace or the crude stone tools made by a human hand more than a million years ago. Perhaps, at the door, our tourist pauses to buy a replica of the archaeological find in the case. It is a pleasing reminder of a fleeting visit to the past, a memento to be displayed to admiring friends at home. But, unfortunately, many people are greedier. They covet the past and want to own a piece of the real thing for themselves.

Collectors and treasure hunters are the curse of archaeology. Many of them regard themselves as legitimate archaeologists. The vanity of our ancestors decreed that they be buried with their riches to accompany them in the afterlife. The greed of their descendants decrees that people today covet these riches. The antiquities dealer and the private collector pay enormous prices for pre-Columbian pots and other fine antiquities looted from otherwise undisturbed sites. Major museums compete to acquire the finest specimens of prehistoric art. The Metropolitan Museum of Art in New York has paid a cool million dollars for a Greek vase.

There seems to be some fundamental human desire to collect things and display them in the privacy of one's home. Collecting is a passion once described as "so violent that it is inferior to love or ambition only in the pettiness of its aims." People collect everything, from barbed wire to beer cans, and many think of archaeology as the acquisition of objects. But when people collect archaeological finds, they are collecting a part of a finite resource that is rapidly vanishing, a unique archive that can never be replaced. Every object they buy or dig from a site is the product of ancient human behavior. This behavior can be partly reconstructed from objects found in the earth, but much of our insight depends on the **contexts** (positions) in time and space in which the objects occur in the ground. Removing an artifact from its context is an irreversible act that cheats us all of knowledge.

Modern archaeology is not treasure hunting, nor is it a fantasy search for lost worlds; *it is the systematic study of humanity in the past*. This general definition includes not only ancient technology and human behavior, but social organization, religious beliefs, and every aspect of human culture.

**Prehistory** is *that portion of human history which extends back before the time of written documents and archives*. Prehistoric archaeologists are the special breed of archaeologists who study human prehistory.


## TYPES OF ARCHAEOLOGY

There are, of course, many types of archaeologists. Many people associate archaeologists with Greek and Roman temples, with Classical statuary and ancient art, with Egyptian pyramids and mummies. Such studies are the work of **Classical archaeologists**. Many are Classical scholars who use archaeological methods to recover data from the ground. Classical archaeologists rely heavily on written sources. For the most part, they concentrate on architecture and the objects they excavate as fine examples of Classical art. Until recently, they have had relatively little interest in the minute economic and social problems that absorb prehistoric archaeologists. But this inclination is changing, as the prehistoric scholars' theories and methods influence archaeologists working on later periods.

**Historical archaeologists** study sites that date to recent, historical times. Some excavate cities like Saxon London or medieval Winchester, which flourished in the dim yet documented past. American historic-site archaeology focuses on pioneer settlements, such as *Colonial Williamsburg,* Spanish missions in the Southwest, or nineteenth-century frontier forts. Scholars at these sites frequently specialize in such objects as pottery imported from England, Italy, and China, Spanish-style architecture, and uniform buttons. Some archaeologists study factories or slum housing dating from the Industrial Revolution or even later.

For each of these projects, the archaeologist supplies details lacking in historical records. Contemporary historical records are usually filled with political and religious matters, with the deeds of civic leaders and statesmen. They rarely describe how people lived, the meals they ate, or where their toilets were located. Hundreds of small cottages were huddled within the walls of medieval Winchester in England. Their owners plied their crafts, quarreled with others, even went to court to settle their differences. Court records and title deeds provide the names of the cottage owners and the details of their law cases. The archaeologist can learn more about them, tracing the long-forgotten foundations of their houses. Much of historical archaeology leads to reconstruction of ruined buildings as part of our national heritage. Colonial Williamsburg, Virginia, is the most famous of early American towns. It has been reconstructed with active help from archaeologists (Figure 1.3).

**Underwater archaeologists** study ancient wrecks in the Mediterranean, around Florida, and elsewhere. Special recording techniques have been devised to recover the smallest details of shipwrecks and the cargoes in their holds. Unfortunately, many people believe that wrecks hold rich treasure and golden doubloons. Thus, many wrecks are robbed or destroyed by inquisitive divers long before archaeologists can get to them. Although people think of underwater archaeology as different from excavation ashore, it is not. Archaeologists working underwater have exactly the same intellectual goals as their dry-land colleagues—to recover, reconstruct, and interpret the past. Their scuba gear and recording and recovery technology for recovering finds are specialized, but they are still studying ancient cultures.

Archaeology has been used to study modern households, too. Using methods developed for studying prehistoric rubbish heaps, archaeologist William Rathje delved into thousands of Tucson, Arizona garbage bags, studying the waste disposal of lower-, middle-, and upper-income households. He found that most people discard rubbish indiscriminately, that low-income families consume the most vitamin pills, and that the average Tucson family wastes about one-hundred dollars' worth of beef a year. The implications of this research for consumers and manufacturers are fascinating. The Tucson project also provided useful theoretical information for study-

FIGURE 1.3 Excavations at Colonial Williamsburg. Historical archaeology was applied here to discover details of a Colonial mental hospital.

ing ancient middens (garbage heaps), even if Tucson itself happens to be several sizes larger than ancient Nineveh or Teotihuacán.

In contrast to Classical and historical archaeologists, **prehistoric archaeologists** deal with an enormous time scale of human cultural evolution that extends back at least 2.3 million years. Prehistoric archaeology is the primary source of information on 99 percent of human history. Prehistoric archaeologists investigate how early human societies all over the world came into being, how they differed from one another, and, in particular, how they changed through time.

The prehistoric archaeologist has to be a specialist in a specific area and time period. No one could possibly become an expert in every aspect of prehistoric archaeology. Some specialists deal with the earliest human beings, working closely with geologists and anthropologists who are interested in human biological evolution. Others are experts in stone toolmaking, in the early peopling of the New and Old Worlds, or in the life-styles of hunter-gatherers. Specialists in the origins of agriculture or urban civilization work closely with experts on topics ranging from architecture to cattle. The best archaeological excavations are those involving a team of scientists cooperating to study prehistoric settlements in the context of their environments. We shall give many examples of this type of research.

## HUMAN PREHISTORY

Until comparatively recent times, scientists believed that the Biblical legend of the Creation was absolutely true, and that God had created the earth in seven days. In the seventeenth century, Archbishop James Ussher calculated from the scriptures that the world was created in 4004 B.C. This timetable left only six thousand years for all of human existence. It was not until 1859 that Charles Darwin's theory of evolution and natural selection provided an alternative explanation for the origins of humankind, allowing a much longer time scale for the presence of human beings on earth.

By that time, too, archaeologists had found crude, humanly made stone axes in the same geological beds as the bones of long-extinct animals. Clearly now, people had been living on earth far longer than six thousand years. But how long had they been around? When and how did the first humans evolve? Was there a "missing link" between humans and apes? The great biologist Thomas Huxley posed the question: "The question of questions for mankind, the problem which underlies all others, and is more deeply interesting than any other—is the ascertainment of the place which man occupies in nature and of his relations to the universe of things."

This was not the only problem. How had early humans settled the world and evolved so many different societies? When the Spaniards reached the New World in the fifteenth century, they came across flourishing human societies that appeared to have been in existence for millennia. The Europeans did not know what to make of these people. (Hernando Cortés and his conquistadors managed to obliterate the remarkable Aztec civilization of Mexico in a few short months.) Some Spaniards questioned whether the Indians were human at all. When it was established that they were, the problem became one of relating them to the Biblical story of the Creation, and the Garden of Eden. Had all humankind descended from one stock? If so, how had the American Indians gotten to the New World?

By the end of the nineteenth century, most scholars agreed that the earliest Americans had probably arrived in the New World via the˙ Bering Strait. But how long ago had they crossed its arctic waters? When did the first *hunter-gatherer* bands settle on the Great Plains and in Patagonia?[2] When archaeologists found stone arrowheads next to the bones of extinct animals in New Mexico in 1924, they knew that early Indians had been hunting large, long-vanished mammals. But still, more than half a century later, no one knows just how long ago the first Americans crossed from Asia.

Many other areas of the world remain as much of a mystery, for the first peopling of the globe is still imperfectly understood. Prehistoric archaeologists are trying to document

[2]Some simple definitions will be helpful.

*Hunter-gatherers:* human societies that lived by hunting wild game, large and small, and by gathering wild vegetable foods, as well as by fishing. Hunting and gathering was the only human lifeway from the earliest prehistoric times up to the development of agriculture and animal domestication in the Near East some 10,000 years ago. Only a handful of hunter-gatherer societies, such as the San of the Kalahari desert, survive to this day.

*Urban:* city-dwelling. Archaeologists have argued for years about how to define a city. In general, cities have more than 5,000 inhabitants and are far more complex entities than villages or towns, especially in their social organization and nonagricultural activities.

*City States:* cities with large, very complex social organizations that controlled specific territories. Satellite settlements throughout this territory provided food and other resources to the controlling city. City states contrast with villages that farmed much smaller areas of land owned by individual kin groups. Early Sumerian civilization flourished over a huge area that is now Iraq between the rivers Tigris and Euphrates. It was made up of dozens of competing city states that controlled much smaller areas of land.

and understand the ways in which humanity adapted itself to the many and diverse environments of the globe. By studying these adaptations, we can begin to understand the astonishing diversity of human cultures that make up our own world.

As archaeologists began to study the prehistory of humankind, a new breed of social scientist, the anthropologist, was beginning to look at the many strange and diverse societies that explorers and missionaries were revealing every year. They ranged from the simple hunter-gatherer societies of the Tierra del Fuego Indians and Australian Aborigines to the more complex and well-organized societies of the Japanese Ainu and the Pueblo Indians of the American Southwest. Then there were the ancient Egyptians and the Sumerians of Mesopotamia, whose societies could be directly linked to early Western civilization. How could one explain all this diversity?

In the 1870s, the great British anthropologist Edward Tylor attempted to do so. He organized humanity into three stages of achievement. The earliest prehistoric bands were obviously hunter-gatherers. He grouped them with modern hunter-gatherers in a state of *Savagery*. Much later, peoples cultivated crops and tamed animals. They moved around less than their predecessors and lived in more elaborate societies. Tylor described such people as being at a stage of *Barbarism*, a far cry from modern civilization, but more advanced culturally than mere Savagery. Tylor considered his own Victorian society to be the ultimate pinnacle that, at least theoretically, all human beings sought to reach. And so he named his most advanced stage *Civilization*. The Sumerians and ancient Egyptians were the earliest of civilizations. Human societies, argued Tylor, had progressed through these stages on their way to modern civilization.

But if some peoples had progressed, how had they first become farmers and cattle herders; how had they become civilized? Both these major developments have been studied intensively since the 1870s, for they are rightly regarded as major milestones in prehistory.

The first scholars to speculate about early agriculture assumed that both the first civilizations and the earliest farmers appeared in the Near East. Therefore they searched for the village occupied by the genius who had first planted the soil and watched precious wheat grains germinate into a new and predictable food supply. No one has ever found this mythical genius. We now realize that farming and the domestication of animals were changes in human culture that took place over thousands of years, not only in the Near East but in other areas of the world as well. Throughout prehistory, human societies experimented with new ideas and technologies. Only a few caught on, and only a handful—among them agriculture, metalworking, writing, and wheeled transport— have radically affected culture.

Even the Greeks and Romans assumed that the ancient Egyptians were the earliest human civilizations. They pointed to the silent pyramids of Giza rising above the banks of the Nile, to the great learning of Egyptian priests. But it was in fact the Mesopotamian delta between the Tigris and Euphrates rivers that saw the world's first city states and urban communities more than five thousand years ago. Sumerian civilization boasted of fine public buildings, great temples and many priests, and a distinctive written script that soon evolved into wedgelike cuneiform writing. From the Sumerians, a continuous historical record takes us from Mesopotamia through Biblical times right up to the conflicts and astonishing economic and technical achievements of Western civilization. Western colonists and missionaries were soon encountering and overwhelming the mighty civilizations of the Aztec and Inca. They befriended and exploited the Virginia Indians and accelerated the extinction of "primitive people" all over the world.

Most prehistoric peoples did not long resist the onslaught of Western civilization. The Tasmanians lasted precisely seventy years before they were hunted into extinction. The Indians of Tierra del Fuego were decimated by whale hunters and disease; they managed to survive until this century, a scant four hundred years after their first encounters with Europeans. Many prehistoric tribes in Africa and the Amazon Basin confronted Western civilization for the first time only within the last century. As fast as Westerners encountered alien societies, they sought to mold them to their own concept of what a "civilized" human society should be. Archaeologists in turn assumed that theirs was the only civilization to create the great inventions of humankind.

The steamship, railroad, automobile, and airplane have revolutionized travel since the early days of archaeology. Most archaeologists love to travel to remote places. As travel became easier, they excavated much farther afield than the narrow horizons of the Near East. The archaeological researchers in this century have revealed an array of prehistoric human societies as varied as the picture of living peoples revealed by eighteenth- and nineteenth-century explorations. People are now beginning to think of a true world prehistory, amplifying and extending written history back into the unknown all over the globe.

We now know that complex prehistoric civilizations flourished by the Indus River in Pakistan, in northern China, and in North America, Mexico, and Peru. The Cretans and Mycenaeans enjoyed a prosperous civilization about 3,500 years ago. African rulers held sway over enormous empires in tropical Africa over the last two thousand years. Few human experiences are unique, and parallel developments in many parts of the world should come as no surprise. No longer can one agree with Edward Tylor and other pioneers that all humankind evolved in well-regimented stages from Savagery through Barbarism to an ultimate state of Civilization.

Only a few of these major developments in human history are adequately recorded in historical archives. The long millennia of human prehistory stretch back into the past from the earlier limits of recorded history in the Near East some five thousand years ago. In many parts of the world, recorded history has an even shorter time scale. The first written records of North American Indian society date from the fifteenth century A.D. The Tahitians of Polynesia first came into written history in A.D. 1767, many African peoples as late as A.D. 1890. Except for some folklore and historical traditions handed down by word of mouth from generation to generation, the only source of information about these, and many other prehistoric peoples, comes from the ground—from long-abandoned settlements and burial sites.

Human prehistory begins with the very earliest concentrations of stone artifacts and animal bones assembled by the first toolmaking human beings some 2.3 million years ago. It extends right up to the beginnings of historic urban civilizations and, in many places, into our own times (Figure 1.4). It is that type of archaeologist known as a prehistoric ar-

| | |
|---|---|
| Modern times | — A.D. 1492; Columbus lands in New World |
| | |
| A.D. 1 | — Teotihuacán, 200 B.C. to A.D. 750 |
| | Maya civilization, *ca.* 200 B.C. |
| 1200 B.C. | — Olmec society in Mexico |
| 1600 B.C. | — Cretan and Mycenaean civilization in Mediterranean |
| | Shang Dynasty in China |
| 2700 B.C. | — Indus civilization in Pakistan |
| | |
| 3000 B.C. | — Cities and civilization in Egypt and Mesopotamia |
| | |
| 6000 B.C. | — Agriculture in the Americas (Tehuacán Valley) |
| 10,000 B.C. | — Agriculture and animal domestication in the |
| | Near East and Southeast Asia |
| 15,000 years ago | — Colonization of the New World (? date uncertain) |
| 40,000 years ago | — Widespread appearance of modern human beings |
| | *(Homo sapiens sapiens)* |
| 40,000 to 1 million years ago | — Hunter-gatherers in the Old World |
| 1.7 million years ago | — Olduvai Gorge |
| 2.3 million years ago | — Earliest tool-making hominids? |
| 4 to 5 million years ago | — Earliest human fossils? |

FIGURE 1.4  Major events in prehistory referred to in this text.

16

chaeologist who studies the major developments of prehistory and places them in accurate temporal and spatial contexts.

## ANTHROPOLOGICAL ARCHAEOLOGY

Anthropology is a discipline for studying humanity in the widest possible sense, both in the past and in the present. Like archaeologists, anthropologists are often thought of as solitary fieldworkers studying primitive tribes in remote jungles or on Pacific islands. Anthropology has a long and distinguished record of such studies conducted by remarkable people like Franz Boas, who worked among the American Indians, Bronislaw Malinowski, who worked in the Trobriand Islands, and many others. Today, however, many types of anthropologists study all manner of specialized topics. **Social anthropologists** primarily work with social organization and the more intangible aspects of human society. Some are specialists, although they may combine their specialty with theoretical insights from social anthropology in the field. **Ethnographers** study technology and economic life, and collect data on social organization and other aspects of human culture. The **ethnologist** generalizes from the information collected by the ethnographer. The **physical anthropologist** studies human biological evolution and the behavior of human beings and their closest relatives. Then there are medical, psychological, urban, and other anthropologists who study aspects of modern industrial and nonindustrial society. Archaeologists are anthropologists as well; their goals are the same as those of their colleagues. But they concentrate on ancient societies, cultures that existed in the past and are now extinct or in existence only in modified form.

The close ties between archaeology and anthropology were demonstrated very dramatically in the southwestern United States a century ago. Swiss-born Adolph Bandelier spent years wandering through the Southwest on a mule. He acquired encyclopedic knowledge of Pueblo Indians and their recent history, both from Indian informants and early Spanish records. He worked back from "the known to the unknown, step by step." This approach remains a basic principle of archaeological research today. Mission records, word-of-mouth histories from tribal historians, modern pottery and ancient potsherds (pot fragments), all were a jigsaw puzzle of information from which the early history of the southwestern Indians was formed. Bandelier regarded archaeology as a means for extending anthropology into the more distant past.

So too did Frank Hamilton Cushing, a pioneer ethnologist who spent five and a half years living among the Zuni Indians in their remote pueblos. He dressed like a Zuni, learned their language, was admitted into their secret societies. Everywhere he looked, he saw a well-organized and long-lived society whose architecture, artifacts, and lifeways stretched far back into the past. Archaeology, he said, was "ethnology carried back into prehistoric times."

When archaeologists began to dig into the long-abandoned pueblos spotted by Bandelier and Cushing, they traced the pottery styles and architectural designs of the pueblos back from modern times into earlier, prehistoric centuries. To do so, they built on Bandelier's work. They excavated and used the many layers of occupation in ancient and modern villages to develop a time scale for prehistoric cultures. And when the famed archaeologist A. V. Kidder dug extensively into *Pecos Pueblo* in New Mexico in 1916, he analyzed thousands of pot fragments and other small finds, constructing an extremely precise time framework of southwestern prehistory that carried these pioneer efforts to their logical conclusion. The theoretical concepts of anthropology, as well as archaeology itself, have subsequently provided a scheme for looking at pre-Columbian Indian cultures, not only in the Southwest, but all over North America (Figures 1.5 and 1.6).

One big message in this book is that archaeology is much more than the study of objects dug up from the ground. As Bandelier, Kidder, and their successors have shown, archaeologists and anthropologists work with the human condition in all its fascinating variety. Archaeologists look at their finds not merely as objects to be examined and admired, but as vital parts of the extinct society that made them. And our ultimate goal, as archaeologists and anthropologists, is to study human society, not objects.

FIGURE 1.5   Pueblo Bonito, New Mexico, a southwestern Pueblo site
dated to A.D. 919–1130. The round structures are kivas, subterranean
ceremonial rooms.

## GOALS OF ARCHAEOLOGY

Anthropological archaeology is commonly agreed to have
three important goals: (1) the study of culture history, (2) the
reconstruction of ancient lifeways, and (3) the investigation
of ways in which human cultures changed in prehistory, and
why.

Our knowledge of **culture history** comes from the study of

FIGURE 1.6   Rain dance at Zuni pueblo. A photograph taken by D. A. Cadzow early in the twentieth century.

archaeological sites, and of the many manufactured tools, houses and other structures, and also food remains found there. Groups of sites and their excavated contents must be described. The archaeologist orders these sites and finds into a time sequence; the distributions of settlements and many objects are plotted on maps and diagrams (Chapter 7). These descriptive operations yield sequences of prehistoric sites and cultures that may cover a few centuries in a valley or thousands of years of prehistoric time in an entire region. Once these sequences are set up in space and time, one has a basis for observing changes in human culture over the years.

In the traditional view of culture history, archaeologists are anthropologists who describe the *surviving remains* of human behavior in the past. Because preservation conditions in the ground are generally poor, only the most durable ot human tools usually survive there. Thus, many archaeologists who share the traditional view of culture history believe that it is pointless to investigate the more intangible aspects of human culture—social organization, religious beliefs, and so on. This belief has led many archaeologists to limit themselves to classifying hundreds of sites and tools. The result is dozens of sequences of carefully ordered sites described in thousands of scientific papers, and museum storerooms full of rows of humanly manufactured tools. These tools, and other objects, have been described like lifeless catalog items rather than being regarded as the products of inventive human minds.

During the 1950s, more and more archaeologists began to realize that this classifying was not enough. They argued that prehistoric societies had undergone major changes as a result of ecological and environmental factors.[3] The many finds they had classified into sequences of human culture gave, at best, a very limited picture of these prehistoric societies. And so they started to look at ways in which people made their living, of exploiting their natural environment. Instead of just examining manufactured tools, they studied broken animal bones, tiny seeds, and other food remains that had survived alongside the artifacts. All these foods had been selected from the natural environment: local environment was a critical backdrop to all human cultures. Environment affected not only food supplies and life-style, but the pattern of human settlement on the landscape as well. The soils, vegetation, water supplies, as well as geography had all helped shape the life-style of the prehistoric inhabitants who exploited it.

One of the first archaeologists to recognize this relationship was Gordon R. Willey, who carried out a pioneer study of human settlement in the Virú Valley, Peru, in 1948. Many months of survey with aerial photographs, on foot, and by jeep showed how the inhabitants of the valley had relied more and more heavily on irrigation agriculture and how their settlements had gradually become larger and more sedentary. Many archaeologists have followed his example, with settlement studies in Mexico, North America, and many parts of Europe and the Near East.

[3]*Ecology:* The study of the relationships between living organisms and their environment.

But the settlement patterns and life-styles of prehistoric societies are, in turn, only part of the picture. Such reconstructions of ancient life-styles described human societies' constant
interactions with an ever-changing natural environment. But
few archaeologists made any attempt to explain *why* the many
changes in prehistoric culture and society they observed took
place.

Then in the 1960s, archaeology underwent a major change
in its methods and theoretical approaches. A new generation
of archaeologists was confronted with an enormous body of
new information from excavations all over the world. They
were trained in applying new scientific research methods and
statistical techniques. They began using computers to store
and manipulate large inventories of data. Part of their training
was influenced by a new body of theoretical concepts developed by philosophers of science. Not content with description, these scholars began to search for explanations of culture change, for the reasons why societies and cultures
evolved in time and space.

These new investigations were spearheaded by archaeologist Lewis Binford, who argued that more rigorous scientific
methods were needed to investigate the past. Very explicit
scientific investigative methods were now called for. These
techniques required careful development of research hypotheses that were to be tested by scientifically collected data.
Binford and his many disciples took archaeology in a new
direction. It was not enough just to describe sites, artifacts,
life-styles, and sequences of human culture. They wanted to
understand *why* human cultures were what they were at different stages of prehistoric time all over the world.

This new approach went even further. Instead of assuming
that preservation conditions would determine the amount of
information that could be obtained about prehistoric societies,
Binford and others began by assuming the opposite—that *all*
aspects of human cultures and societies, whether material objects or intangibles (like religious beliefs), are preserved (indirectly, perhaps) in archaeological sites, and can be fully
recorded. But to recover the more intangible aspects of human society, extremely rigorous methods and precisely formulated research designs were essential. Not only could one
recover information about religious and social organization,

but one could also develop hypotheses about the very processes that led to changes in human cultures in the past. These hypotheses could be tested against archaeological evidence. Thus, they argued, archaeology is far more than a descriptive subdiscipline of anthropology: it is a science, using scientific methods not only to describe the past, but to explain it as well.

Ten years ago, archaeologists were talking about a "new archaeology." Carried away with enthusiasm for the scientific approach, they believed the new approach would overcome many of archaeology's problems with incomplete preservation of the past. That talk has died down, for the "new" archaeology is now far from new, and the promised breakthroughs have failed to materialize. Today, many archaeologists are again searching for a new body of archaeological theory that truly will provide us with new models for interpreting the past.

Some scholars are searching for the "meaning" of the archaeological record, for ancient ideologies, for the *structure* of prehistoric societies. To do so, they have borrowed theoretical concepts and models from cultural anthropology. Archaeologists studying **structural archaeology** believe that prehistoric people were like actors, in that they created, used, and manipulated their symbolic capabilities to make and remake the world they lived in. Thus, the meaning of a prehistoric society's world was more important than its material achievements. Unlike "new" archaeologists, then, one cannot interpret the past only by ecological, technological, and other material artifacts. Furthermore, this school of thought believes that archaeology is not an objective, scientific discipline. Nor is it a luxury. The past is a social creation, they argue, and so archaeologists must answer the question: why is their interpretation of the past the only correct one? They see archaeology as a social construct, as much part of our culture as language. Some archaeologists of a Marxist persuasion even go as far as to argue along with Marx that history is always created in the service of "class interests." Under this argument, archaeologists should regard the past as ideology.

Structural archaeologists seek to investigate the codes and rules according to which the observed relationships between parts of cultural systems come into being. They try to get at the active, social manipulation of symbols, objects as they are perceived by their owners, not merely at their use in the past. The concept of structural archaeology is all very well in theory, but few archaeological studies have yet provided convincing accounts of the relationships between the "codes" and social and ecological organization. Only a few researches have produced insights into the structure of prehistoric societies, most of them carried out with the aid of written texts. David Freidel and Linda Schele have used Maya sculptures and hieroglyphic symbols to trace changes in the meanings of symbols associated with political power. They have shown how the planet Venus and the Sun were critical elements in Maya religious belief, so much so that rulers came to erect temples and other monuments that legitimized their identity with the gods and validated their rule.

Where does the future lie? Large-scale archaeological researches in Mexico, the Southwest, and elsewhere have shown that archaeology is an unrivaled way of studying human cultural evolution in the remote past. So far, it lacks its own body of original theory, but it shares many problems with evolutionary biology. Both disciplines face the same problem: How do forms, whether living or cultural, come into being and stabilize? Clearly, archaeology's intellectual future is tied to current, dramatic advances in biology—and to our own perceptions of the role archaeology has to play in the twentieth-century world.

# 2

# CULTURE AND THE ARCHAEOLOGICAL RECORD

An archaeologist of 6666 A.D. may find himself
obliged to rely on the divergences between assemblages of kitchen utensils to help him recognize that
by 1950, the United Kingdom and United States of
America were not occupied by the same society.

v. GORDON CHILDE, 1956


## HUMAN CULTURE

Everyone lives within a cultural context, one that is qualified by a label like "middle-class American," "Roman," or
"Sioux." These labels conjure up characteristic objects or behavior patterns typical of this culture. We associate ham-
burgers with middle-class American culture and skin kayaks
with Eskimos. Romans are thought to have spent their time
conquering the world, Sioux wandering over the Great Plains.
But our stereotypes are often crude, inaccurate generalizations. We think of Native Americans as legendary, feathered
braves, but only a few Indian groups ever wore such head-
dresses. In fact, the label "American Indian" includes incredibly diverse peoples, ranging from family-size hunter-gatherer bands to large, complex civilizations.

Each human society has its recognizable cultural style,
which shapes the behavior of its members, their political and
judicial institutions, and their morals. Every traveler is familiar with the distinctive "flavor" of various cultures that we
experience when dining in a foreign restaurant or arriving in
a strange country. This distinctiveness results from a people's
complex adaptation to greatly varied ecological, societal, and
cultural factors.

Human culture is unique because much of its content is transmitted from generation to generation by sophisticated communication systems. Formal education, religious beliefs, and day-to-day social intercourse all transmit culture and allow societies to develop complex and continuing adaptations to aid their survival. Such communication systems also help rapid cultural change to take place, as when less advanced societies come into contact with more advanced ones. Culture is a potential guide for our behavior created through generations of human experience. It provides a design for living that helps mold our responses to different situations.

We human beings are the only animals to use our culture as the primary means of adapting to our environment. Although biological evolution has protected the polar bear from arctic winters, only human beings make thick clothes and snow igloos in the Arctic and live in light, thatched shelters in the tropics. Culture is an adaptive system; it is an interface between ourselves, the environment, and other human societies. Through the long millennia of prehistory, human culture became more elaborate. If this cultural buffer were now removed, we would be helpless and most probably doomed to extinction. As our only means of adaptation, human culture is always adjusting to environmental, technological, and societal change.

Culture can be subdivided in many ways. Language, economics, technology, religion, and political and social organization are but a few of the interacting elements. These elements shape one another and blend to form a whole. The distribution of water and food supplies, as well as flexible social organization, helps determine the distribution of home bases among the San of the Kalahari Desert in southern Africa.

Culture is the dominant factor in determining social behavior; human society is the vehicle that carries our culture. **Societies** are groups of interacting organizers. Insects and other animals, as well as humans, have societies. But only humans have culture as well.

What is *culture?* Anthropologists have tried to define this most elusive of theoretical formulations for generations. All such definitions are concepts that are a means of explaining cultures and human behavior in terms of the shared ideas a group of people may hold. One of the best definitions was written by the great Victorian anthropologist Sir Edward Tylor more than a century ago. He wrote that culture is "That complex whole which includes knowledge, belief, art, morals, law, custom, and any other capabilities and habits acquired by man as a member of society." To that definition, modern archaeologists would add the statement that culture is our primary means of adapting to our environment.

The concept of culture provides anthropological archaeologists with a means for explaining the products of human activity. When archaeologists study the tangible remains of the past, they see a patterned reflection of the culture that produced them, of the shared behavior of a group of prehistoric people. This **patterning** of archaeological finds is critical, for it reflects patterned behavior in the past.

## CULTURAL SYSTEMS

Many of the interacting components of culture are highly perishable. So far, no one has been able to dig up a religious philosophy or an unwritten language. Archaeologists have to work with the *tangible* remains of human activity that still survive in the ground. But these surviving remains of human activity are radically affected by *intangible* aspects of human culture. The Hopewell people of the American Midwest traded finely made ornaments fashioned of hammered copper sheet (Figure 2.1) over enormous distances 1,800 years ago. These ornaments turn up in Hopewell burial mounds. The copper technology that made them was simple, but the symbolism behind the artifacts was not. They were probably exchanged between important individuals as symbolic gifts, denoting kin ties, economic obligations, and other social meanings that are beyond the archaeologist's ability to recover. Thus, the artifacts found in an excavation reflect not only ancient technology, but the values and uses that a society placed on such objects. Ancient tools are not culture in themselves, but they are a patterned reflection of the culture that produced them. Archaeologists spend much time studying the linkages between past cultures and their archaeological remains.

FIGURE 2.1  Hopewell raven or crow in beaten copper.

Anthropologist Leslie White was one of the first to study peoples' means of adapting to their environment. He argued that *human culture is made up of many structurally different parts which articulate with one another within a total cultural system* (Figure 2.2). This cultural system is the means whereby a human society adapts to its physical and social environment.

All cultural systems articulate with other systems, which also are made up of interacting sets of variables. One such system is the natural environment. The links between cultural and environmental systems are such that a change in one system is linked to changes in the other. Thus, a major objective of archaeology is to understand the linkage between the various parts of cultural and environmental systems as they are reflected in archaeological data. It follows that archaeologists studying cultural systems are more interested in the *relationships* between activities and tools within a cultural system than they are in the activities or tools themselves. They are profoundly interested in cultural systems within their environmental context.

To be workable, any human cultural system depends on its ability to adapt to the natural environment. A cultural system can be broken down into all manner of subsystems: religious and ritual subsystems, economic subsystems, and so on. Each of these is linked to the others. Changes in one subsystem, such as a shift from cattle herding to wheat growing, will cause reactions in many others. Such relationships give the archaeologist a measure of the constant changes and varia-

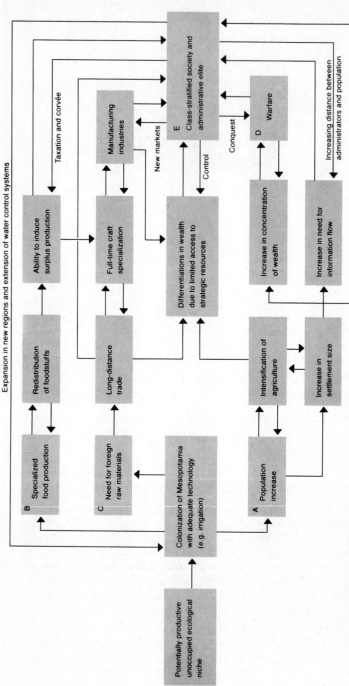

FIGURE 2.2 Cultural systems are, of course, theoretical formulations used by archaeologists to interpret the past. This systems model illustrates a systems approach to understanding human culture. It is an attempt to document the relationships between cultural and environmental variables that led to state-organized societies in Mesopotamia between 5,000 and 2,000 B.C. (From *The Rise of Civilization* by Charles L. Redman. Copyright © 1978 W. H. Freeman and Company. Reprinted with permission.)

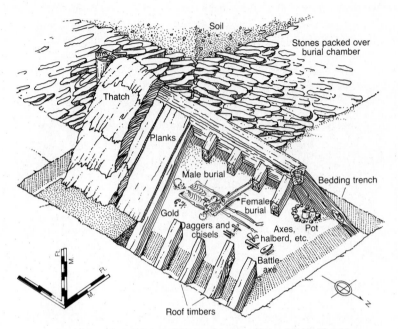

Soil

Stones packed over burial chamber

Thatch

Planks

Male burial

Gold

Daggers and chisels

Female burial

Bedding trench

Axes, Pot halberd, etc.

Battle-axe

Roof timbers

FIGURE 2.3 A wooden burial house from Leubingen, East Germany. The two burials were deposited in a wooden house under a mound. The archaeologist recovers not only the burials, and the objects with which they were buried, but also reconstructs the burial layout and sequence of construction of the burial house. Further, the archaeologist tries to infer the funerary rituals from the artifact patterning and the structures under the mound.

tions in human culture that can accumulate over long periods. These changes accumulate as cultural systems respond to external and internal stimuli.

By examining the systematic patternings of archaeological finds, we can discover more about the intangible aspects of human behavior. By dropping their possessions on the ground or burying their dead in certain ways, people have left vital information about many more elements in their cultural system than merely their tools or skeletal remains (Figure 2.3). One can examine the relationship between individual households by comparing the artifacts left by each; one can study trading practices by analyzing the products of metalsmiths; one can discover religious beliefs by mapping temple architecture. Also, the carefully arranged grave offerings in a royal cemetery tell us much about the ranked members of a royal court buried in a communal grave. And the precise and sophisticated recovery of such data is crucial for analysis and interpretation in modern prehistoric archaeology.

## CULTURAL PROCESS

Every cultural system is in a constant state of change. Its various political, social, and technological subsystems adjust to changing circumstances. We ourselves live in a time of rapid cultural change, in which measurable differences set apart different ten-year periods. We would find it hard to identify the thousands of minor daily, cultural changes that occur, but we can easily recognize the cumulative affects of these minor changes over a longer period.

Consider the many minor changes in automobile design over the past decade, which in themselves are not very striking. But if one looks at the *cumulative* effect of ten years' steady change toward safer cars—energy-absorbing bumpers, padded steering wheels and dashboards, seat belts, fewer projecting ornaments—the change is striking. The automobile of today is different from that of the 1970s, and many of the changes are due to tighter governmental safety regulations, which in turn are due to greater public safety consciousness. Here we see a major cumulative change in part of our enormous technological subsystem. By examining the relationship between technological and political subsystems, as in this example, we can understand the processes by which culture changed.

The word *process* implies a patterned sequence of events, one event leading to another. A three-bedroom house is built in an ordered sequence of events, from foundation footings up to final painting. (Archaeological research itself has a process—research design and formulating hypotheses; collecting, and interpreting, data to test those hypotheses; publishing the results.) To analyze cultural process, we consider all the factors that cause changes in human culture and how they affect one another.

How did human cultures change in the past? What cultural processes came into play when people began to cultivate the soil, or when complex and elaborate urban states developed five thousand years ago? As we saw in Chapter 1, at first students of the past thought that major inventions like agriculture had been devised by a lone genius. The new discoveries were thought to have spread throughout the world by mass migrations, or by long-distance trading over continents and oceans. But as more and more archaeological data have accumulated in all corners of the world, people have realized that such straightforward explanations of cultural process as universal evolution, or the spread of all ideas from one place of invention, are simplistic and do not reflect actual reality.

Most changes in human culture have been cumulative, occurring slowly, over a long time. Processes of culture change in prehistory were the result of constantly changing adaptations to myriad external environments. Cultural systems were constantly adjusting and evolving in response to feedback from both inside and outside.

Clearly, no one element in a cultural system is a primary cause of culture change, because a complex range of factors—rainfall, vegetation, technology, social restrictions, and population density, to mention only a few—interact with one another and react to a change in any element in the system. From the ecologist's point of view, therefore, human culture is merely one element in the ecosystem, a mechanism whereby people adapt to this environment. This viewpoint provides a useful framework for much modern archaeological research, and for studying cultural process.

We shall look more closely at ways in which people have sought to interpret cultural process in prehistory in Chapter 7.

## THE ARCHAEOLOGICAL RECORD

Prehistoric archaeologists study ancient human behavior by way of the traces of such behavior that survive in food remains, structures, and humanly manufactured objects. These material remains form the **archaeological record**, the archives of human history before written records.

The archaeological record comprises all kinds of archaeological finds, from the pyramids of Giza to an early human campsite at Olduvai Gorge, Tanzania, occupied nearly two million years ago. California shell mounds, Ohio earthworks, Inca cemeteries, all are part of the archaeological record. So too are isolated artifacts—the throne of Tutankhamun, a wooden religious mask from a midwestern burial mound, or a Polynesian stone adze.

We seek to find out about prehistoric people from the traces of their activities. The butchered carcass of a mammoth slaughtered twenty thousand years ago is a mine of information on ancient hunting practices. Analysis of dried-out seeds or ancient human body waste found in archaeological sites tell us much about prehistoric diet.

What we can find out about the past is severely limited, it is true, by the state of preservation of archaeological finds. Some substances such as baked clay or stone will survive indefinitely. But wood bone, leather, and other organic materials soon vanish except under waterlogged, frozen, or exceptionally dry conditions. Everyone has heard of the remarkable tomb of Egyptian pharaoh Tutankhamun ("King Tut"), whose astonishing treasure survived almost intact in the dry climate of the Nile Valley for more than three thousand years (Figure 2.4). This archaeological record is exceptionally complete and informative. We even know, from the bouquet of wildflowers laid on his inner coffin, that Tutankhamun's funeral took place in the spring.

But most archaeological sites are found where only a few durable materials survive. Constructing the past from these finds is a challenge, the sort of problem faced by the detective piecing together the circumstances of a crime from a few fragmentary clues. The analogy is close: Take two spark plugs, a fragment of a china cup, a needle, a grindstone, and a candlestick. Imagine someone from Patagonia digging them up in a thousand years' time and trying to tell you how the makers *used* the objects. This analysis is precisely what the archaeologist does in going about the work of being a special type of anthropologist.

FIGURE 2.4 The throne of Tutankhamun, one of the many wood artifacts recovered from the richest royal sepulcher ever found.

The data we amass from **survey** (looking for sites) and **excavation** (digging) make up the archaeological record. The two basic units studied by archaeologists are **sites** and **artifacts**.

## Site-Formation Processes

The archaeological record is, of course, incomplete. Many items of material culture, especially such organic items as wood artifacts and baskets, have been lost to decay and destruction. Our interpretations of the record depend on how closely the surviving artifacts represent the total material culture.

All archaeological remains are modified by the passage of time. Archaeologists call the ways in which the archaeological record was formed, *after* a site was abandoned, **site-formation processes.** These are normally local processes and can vary from site to site, even layer to layer: many factors affect how they work. Large artifacts are less likely to be transported by flood water. Easily replaced items such as stone flake knives may be abandoned, unlike treasured ceremonial artifacts or heirlooms. Modern plowing or trampling by cattle, even pressure from human feet can shift the position of quite large artifacts in the ground. So too can earthworms, wind, and carnivores such as scavenging hyenas, to say nothing of the depth of sediments that may cover archaeological remains, or even the density of artifacts in a deposit.

How sites are formed is still little understood, for archaeologists have only just realized how extensively these processes altered archaeological sites as we see them today. They matter because the scattered stone tools and bones you excavate in an archaeological site may represent the remains of a prehistoric butchering. They might also, in fact, have been arranged in this grouping by natural, quite fortuitous actions such as flooding. Much may have changed during the large gap of time we must bridge between the moment when a site was abandoned centuries or thousands of years ago and today, when archaeologists excavate what remains. Archaeologists are assembling a new body of theory to fill this hiatus (Chapter 10).

## Archaeological Sites

Archaeology is based on the scientific recovery of data from the ground, on the systematic excavation and recording of the archaeological record. The **archaeological site** is a place where traces of ancient human activity are to be found. It is the archaeologist's archive, in much the same way as government files can yield a day-by-day record of historical events. Sites are normally identified through the humanly manufactured tools, or artifacts, found in them.

Archaeological sites can range in size from a huge prehistoric city like Teotihuacán, in the Valley of Mexico, to a small campsite occupied by hunter-gatherers at Olduvai Gorge, Tanzania. An archaeological site can consist of a human burial, a huge rockshelter occupied over millennia, or a simple scatter of stone tools found on the surface at the bottom of Death Valley, California. Sites are limited in number and variety by preservation conditions and by the activities of the people who occupied them. Some were used for a few short hours, others for a generation or two. Some, like Mesopotamian city mounds, were major settlements for hundreds, even thousands, of years and contain many separate occupation layers. Great mounds like that of *Ur-of-the-Chaldees* in Mesopotamia contain many occupation levels, which tell the story of a long-established, ancient city that was abandoned when the river Euphrates changed its course away from the settlement.

Archaeological sites are most commonly classified according to the activities that occurred there. Thus, cemeteries and other sepulchers like Tutankhamun's tomb are referred to as burial sites. A 20,000-year-old Stone Age site in the Dnieper Valley of the Ukraine, with mammoth-bone houses, hearths, and other signs of domestic activity, is a **habitation site**. So too are many other sites, such as caves and rockshelters, early Mesoamerican farming villages, and Mesopotamian cities—in all, people live and carried out greatly diverse activities. **Kill sites** consist of bones of slaughtered game animals and the weapons that killed them. They are found in East Africa and on the North American Great Plains. **Quarry sites** are another type of specialist site, where people mined stone or metals to make specific tools. Prized raw materials, such as obsidian, a volcanic glass used for fine knives, were widely traded in prehistoric times and profoundly interest the archaeologist. Then there are such spectacular **religious sites** as the stone circles of Stonehenge in southern England, the Temple of Amun at Karnak, Egypt, and the great ceremonial precincts

FIGURE 2.5  Temple I at Tikal, Guatemala, dating to about A.D. 700, part of a religious site.

of lowland Maya centers in Central America at *Tikal*, Copán, and Palenque (Figure 2.5). **Art sites** are common in southwestern France, southern Africa, and parts of North America, where prehistoric people painted or engraved magnificent displays of art (see Figure 8.5, p. 169). Some French art sites are more than twenty thousand years old.

Each of these site types carries down a form of human activity, which is represented in the archaeological record by specific artifact patterns and surface indications found and recorded by the archaeologist.

## Artifacts

**Artifacts** are objects found in archaeological sites that exhibit features resulting from human activity. The word covers every form of archaeological find, from stone axes to gold ornaments, houses, and other structures, as well as food remains such as broken bones. Artifacts are distinguished from nonartifacts simply because artifacts display patterns of humanly caused features, or attributes.[1] These objects can be classified according to their distinctive attributes. Artifacts are the product of human ideas, ideas that people had about the way objects should look. Every culture has its own rules, which limit and dictate the form of artifacts. Our own society has definite ideas of what a fork should look like, or an automobile, or a pair of shoes. We are so familiar with the artifacts of other cultures that, seeing a skin kayak, we at once identify it as "Eskimo."

Most craft skills such as stone toolmaking, pottery manufacture, basketry, and metallurgy are learned by each new generation. The skills are transmitted from one generation to the next, usually resulting in relatively slow, sometimes very slow, changes in artifacts and artifact technology. This inborn conservatism, which we might call tradition, strongly influences perpetuation of artifact forms.

The variation in a group of similar artifacts, such as stone projectile points, may reflect varied ideas behind them. Archaeologists study and classify artifacts, as we discuss in Chapter 7. These classifications are really research devices, by means of which we study the products of human behavior and, indirectly, human behavior itself.

For the archaeologist, every artifact has a number of **attributes**, identifiable features that combine to give the object its distinctive form. The pots illustrated in Figure 2.6 have several obvious attributes: different painted motifs, rounded bases, handles, and so on. Each of these attributes contributes

---

[1]In this book, an artifact is a formal tool. Elsewhere in archaeological literature the word is often given broader meaning.

FIGURE 2.6   Painted vessels from the American Southwest. Each of these pots has distinctive attributes, some of which it shares with others, others of which are unique. Attributes include rim shape, height, paint colors, design motifs, clay composition, and so on.

to the form of the pot and was part of the mental template that produced it. Each attribute has a different reason for being there. The band of decoration is purely ornamental, part of the decorative tradition among the people who made it. The shape of the pot is determined by its function. It was designed for carrying liquids and for cooking, for which a bag-shaped, round-bottomed body is essential. Attributes can be present because of traditional, functional, technological, or other reasons. Just occcasionally a new attribute will appear, a new decorative motif perhaps, which may vanish just as fast as it appeared. Why? Because it did not catch on with other potmakers. Just occasionally, too, a new attribute may achieve wide popularity and be adopted by everyone. Then the innovation becomes part of the pottery tradition. But the forms of pots among neighboring peoples may be completely different.

The archaeologist is deeply intent on the ways in which artifacts vary and on the changing forms of the many manufactured objects found in archaeological sites. Variation in the form of artifacts is a complex subject, but critical to archaeologists. It is the cumulative results of thousands of minor changes in dozens of artifacts that provide the tangible evidence for culture change in the prehistoric past. And that, as we have seen, is a major interest of anyone studying world prehistory.

## CONTEXT

Artifacts are found in archaeological sites. Archaeological sites are far more than just a collection of artifacts, however. They can hold the remains of dwellings, burials, storage pits, craft activities, and sometimes several occupation levels. Each artifact, each broken bone or tiny seed, every dwelling, has a relationship in space and time to all the other finds made in the site. An artifact can be earlier, contemporary with, or later than its neighbors in the soil. A thousand obsidian flakes and half-completed projectile heads scattered over an area several square feet in diameter are, in themselves, merely stone fragments. But the patterning of all the fragments is significant, for it tells us something of the various manufacturing activities carried out by the person who flaked the thousand fragments from chunks of obsidian. In this instance, and many others, the **context** of the artifacts in time and space is vital.

To every archaeologist, an artifact is worthless without this context. The museums and art galleries of the world are filled with magnificent artifacts that have been collected under circumstances that can only be described as highly unscientific. Generations of treasure hunters have ravaged ancient Egyptian cemeteries and dug up thousands of pre-Columbian pots for museums and private collectors. Few of these objects have any archaeological context. Any expert can look at a pre-Columbian pot and say at once, "Classic Maya." But, tragically, rarely will our expert be able to consult excavation records and say, "Classic Maya, Level VIB from Temple of the Inscriptions, Palenque, excavation C, 1976, associated with burial of an adult male, thirty-five years old, date about A.D. 680." An artifact removed from its context in space and time in an archaeological site is merely an object. An artifact carefully excavated from a recorded archaeological context is an integral part of our history, and as such has far more significance. This context of space and time lies at the very foundations of modern archaeology. We must now look at ways in which we tell how old something is, and what its spatial associations may be.

# 3

## TIME

> What seest thou else in the dark backward and
> abysm of time?
>
> WILLIAM SHAKESPEARE, *The Tempest*

This chapter is about time, about the ways in which archaeologists date projectile points and all the other myriad finds that come from their excavations and surveys.

Human prehistory spans at least two million years of cultural evolution, a vast landscape of sites with long-abandoned food remains, artifacts, burials, and prehistoric dwellings. Each of these sites and their contents has a precise context in time, and an exact position in space as well. Some sites, like the great city of Teotihuacán in Mexico, were occupied for hundreds of years. Other localities, such as Olduvai Gorge, were inhabited for hundreds of thousands. The chronology of prehistory world-wide is made up from thousands of careful excavations and many types of dating tests, used to develop hundreds of local sequences of occupation layers and archaeological sites. Without dates, prehistory would be a jumble of confusing sites and cultures devoid of order.

Our lives are governed by time—by working hours and tax deadlines, bus schedules and precise calendars. Everyone in our society needs access to a timepiece, simply to keep up with everyone else. Precise time measurement is, however, a recent phenomenon. Accurate historical records extend back only five thousand years, to the beginning of ancient Egyptian and Mesopotamian civilizations. Both these societies developed calendars and astronomical predictions to a fine art. The Maya peoples of Mesoamerica devised an astronomically based calendar that they used to precisely regulate cycles of years upon which the prosperity of society depended.

Looking earlier than 3000 B.C., however, we enter a chronological vacuum, a blank that archaeologists have labored to fill with carefully assembled sequences of sites and artifacts. Except in a very few areas such as the American Southwest, where tree rings can be used to date prehistoric sites very accurately, prehistoric times must be measured in centuries and millennia, rather than individual years. We know that Washington, D.C. was founded in A.D. 1800. We will be lucky if we can ever date the beginnings of Teotihuacán to closer than 200 ± 100 years B.C. Some idea of the scale of the problem can be gained by piling up a hundred quarters. If the entire pile represents the time that humankind has been on earth, the length of time covered by historical records will be considerably less than the thickness of one quarter. Ninety-nine and nine-tenths percent of human experience lies in prehistoric times. Small wonder time is important in archaeology.

## RELATIVE CHRONOLOGY

Every event or object has a time relationship to other events and objects. If I place a book on a table, and then pile another on top of it, clearly the upper one of the two was placed on the table after—at a later moment in time than—the original volume. The second book became part of the pile after the first, but how long afterward we have no means of telling. This example illustrates the principle of superposition, the cornerstone of **relative chronology**.

**Superposition**, the notion that underlying levels are earlier than those which cover them, came to archaeology from geology. The geological layers of the earth are superimposed one upon another almost like layers of a cake. Easily viewed examples are cliffs by the seashore or road cuts along the highway, which show a series of geological levels. Obviously, any object deposited in the lower horizons usually got there before the upper strata were accumulated. In other words, the lower levels are relatively earlier than the later strata. The deposition of a series of occupation levels or geological strata in order can be achieved by many processes; wind, water, earthquakes, and other factors. Superposition is fundamental to the study of archaeological sites, for many settlements, such as desert caves in western North America, or Near Eastern mounds, were occupied more or less continuously for hundreds, even thousands, of years. Human occupation of any site results in the accumulation of all kinds of rubbish. Objects are lost and become imbedded in the ground. Buildings fall into disrepair and are leveled to make way for new ones. A flood may wipe out a village and deposit a thick layer of silt. A new village may rise on the same spot years later. The sequence of these superimposed occupation levels is carefully recorded as the excavation of a site proceeds. Of course, not all settlements were occupied several times. Single-occupation sites, even very temporary camps, are studied just as carefully.

The sequence of natural and humanly accumulated layers on an archaeological site is the basis for all stratigraphic observations in archaeology. But as Figure 3.1 shows, it is not only the carefully observed layers, but their detailed contents as well, which provide us with relative chronology. Each level in a settlement has its associated artifacts, objects that the archaeologist uses as indicators of technological, economic social, or even religious change.

## Artifacts and Relative Chronology

Manufactured artifacts are the fundamental data archaeologists use to study past human behavior. These artifacts have changed with passing time in radical ways. One has only to look at the humble stone chopper of the earliest humans and compare it with the latest electric carving knife to get the point. Most artifact changes in prehistory are extremely small; minor changes in such characteristics as the shape, decoration, or lip angle of clay pots accumulate slowly as they ultimately lead to a vessel form that is hardly recognizable as originating from its ancestors.

Archaeologists, like the celebrated Egyptologist Flinders Petrie, have long been fascinated by the gradual changes in artifacts. Petrie, who worked on a huge prehistoric cemetery at Diospolis Parva, Egypt, in 1902, was confronted with the

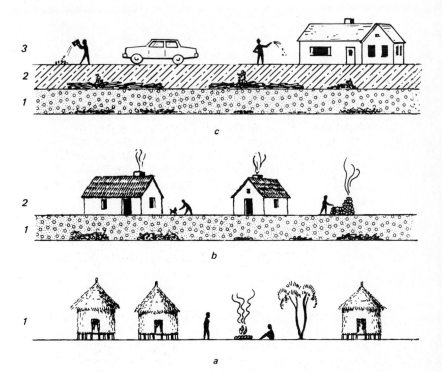

FIGURE 3.1 The principle of superposition. (a) A farming village flourishes 5,000 years ago. After a time, the village is abandoned and the huts fall into disrepair. Their ruins are covered by accumulating earth and vegetation. (b) After an interval, a second village is built on the same site, with different architectural styles. This village in turn is abandoned; the houses collapse into piles of rubble and are covered by accumulating earth. (c) Twentieth-century people park their cars on top of both village sites and drop litter and coins that, when uncovered, reveal to the archaeologist that the top layer is modern.

An archaeologist digging this site would find that the modern layer is underlain by two prehistoric occupation levels, that square houses were in use in the upper of the two, which is the later (law of superposition), and that round huts are stratigraphically earlier than square ones here. Therefore, village 1 is earlier than village 2, but when either was occupied or how many years separate village 1 from 2 cannot be known without further data.

problem of arranging a large number of tombs in chronological order. He eventually placed them in sequence by studying the groups of pots buried with each skeleton, arranging the vessels in such a way that features like handle design reflected gradual change. The earliest handles were useful for lifting the pot. But the latest vessels bore no handles at all, merely painted lines that represented the once useful handle. Petrie used his pots to create a series of "sequence dates," each characterized by a vessel form. Whenever a vessel form similar to Petrie's was found anywhere in Egypt, the pot itself and the objects found with it could be dated within his series. So effective was this relative chronology based on artifacts that it was used for many years.

Recent studies of changing artifacts are based on the assumption that the popularity of any artifact is a fleeting thing. The miniskirt becomes the midi or the maxi; clothing styles change from month to month. Records hit the Top Forty but are forgotten in a short time. Other artifacts have a far longer life. The stone choppers of the earliest humans were a major element in early toolkits (a toolkit is a basic set of tools used by a culture) for hundreds of thousands of years. People used candles for centuries before they turned to kerosene and gas lamps. But each has its period of maximum popularity, or frequency of occurrence, whether it lasts for millennia or only a few months. Figure 3.2 shows how each distribution of artifacts, when plotted, has a profile that has been described as resembling a large battleship's hull viewed from above.

The relatively unsophisticated methods used by Flinders Petrie have been refined into sophisticated **seriation** (ordering) **techniques**. They are based on the assumption that the popularity of pottery types, stone artifact forms, and other objects peaks at a specific moment in time. If we plot the frequencies with which these objecjts occur as a set of bars, they will look like the hull of a battleship glimpsed from an aircraft (Figure 3.2). The center of the hull bulges outward where the armor is thickest, coinciding with the period of greatest popularity. This phenomenon is sometimes called the "battleship curve." Thus, it is argued, when sites within a restricted geographic area contain similar pottery and other artifacts at an equivalent rate of popularity, then they are of approximately the same age. If the samples are statistically

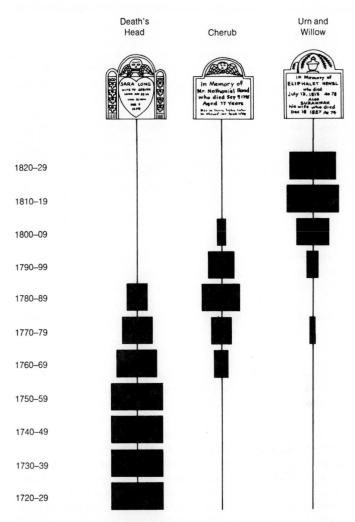

FIGURE 3.2 Seriation. The changing styles of New England grave-stones, from Stoneham, Massachusetts, between 1720 and 1829, ser-iated in three styles. Notice how each style rises to a peak of maxi-mum popularity and then declines as another comes into fashion. The cherub style shows the "classic battleship curve." Each horizontal bar represents the percentage of a gravestone type at that date; e.g., between 1720 and 1729, Death's heads were at 100 percent.

reliable, a series of sites can be linked in a relative chronology, even though, without dates in years, one cannot tell when they were occupied.

Edwin Dethlefsen and James Deetz tested this "battleship-curve" assumption against the changing decorative styles on gravestones in New England Colonial cemeteries. They found that the changing styles of death's heads, cherubs, and urns succeeded one another in an almost perfect series of battleship curves. The dates of the gravestones were known from their inscriptions, and so the experiment could be conducted and tested within a precise chronological context.

A series of archaeological sites may contain many different artifacts that appear and vanish over relatively short periods. By applying seriation, it is possible to place the different forms of artifacts in a series of relative chronologies, like that from the Tehuacán Valley in Mexico illustrated in Figure 3.3. Each occupation level of each site will contain different proportions of each artifact form manufactured at that period. And once you have a sequence of changing artifact frequencies, it is possible to fit isolated, newly discovered sites into your relative chronology.

## Cross-Dating

Seriation is effective for **cross-dating** sites as well. As we have seen, it can be used to assign a newly discovered settlement to a precise position in the relative chronology of a well-studied area, as Flinders Petrie did. In some cases, too, a series of sites may contain objects such as European coins whose date of minting is known. Hence, we have access to dates in years. Let us assume that an English coin dating to 1825 is traded into a California Indian village from far away. The coin falls onto a hut floor and is lost in the dust. in the 1980s, archaeologists find this dated coin in a stratified level of the ancient village. They know it was traded into the settlement *no earlier than its date of minting,* and so the village was flourishing in, or after, 1825. They may find more sites with the same Indian artifacts in similar proportions—but no coins—a few miles away. When they seriate the finds, they will be able to cross-date the undated settlements, because their artifact frequencies are the same. This cross-dating tech-

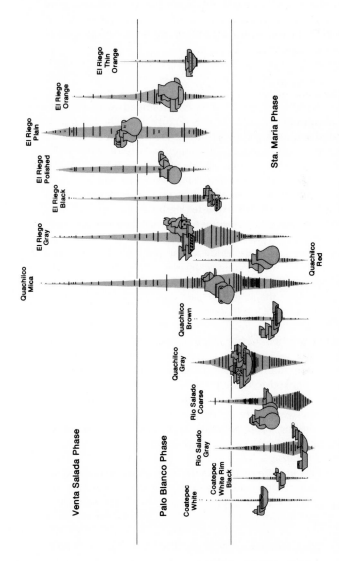

FIGURE 3.3 Seriation of pottery styles from the Tehuacán Valley, Mexico, showing many sites ordered into a single sequence.

51

nique has been widely applied to central European prehistoric sites, whose inhabitants traded with literate civilizations in the Mediterranean basin, exchanging copper and other raw materials for ornaments and other luxuries whose age in years is known.

## Relative Chronology and the Ice Age

The story of human prehistory has unfolded against a backdrop of massive climatic changes (Figure 3.4). The Ice Age or *Pleistocene* is the most recent of the great geological epochs, sometimes called the Age of Humanity. It is remarkable for dramatic swings in world climate. On numerous occasions during the Pleistocene, great ice sheets covered much of western Europe and North America, bringing arctic climate to vast areas of the northern hemisphere (Figure 3.4b). These climatic fluctuations have been documented from deep-sea sediment cores from the world's oceans. Minute foraminifera (protozoa) in these cores are evidence of periods of cooler and warmer ocean waters that coincided with major climatic changes ashore.

At least three major glacial periods settled over the earth during the past 600,000 years, the most recent beginning about 100,000 years ago. They were separated by prolonged periods of warmer climate when temperatures were as warm as, if not warmer than, today's. Traces of human settlement are sometimes found in association with geological deposits that can be linked to these periods of warmer climate. Stone Age sites are common in European river valleys after 400,000 years ago, places where people threw down their stone tools after butchering hippopotamus and other large mammals during millenia when such warmth-loving animals flourished in northern Europe.

Geologists are still trying to puzzle out the complicated sequence of warm and cold periods during the Pleistocene. But we do know that the last glaciation affected northern Europe and North America between about 100,000 and 10,000 years ago. This was a crucial period in prehistory, for then *Homo sapiens sapiens*, modern humanity, differentiated from earlier human stock. Within a surprisingly short time, *Homo sapiens* had peopled Australia, arctic latitudes, and the Americas.

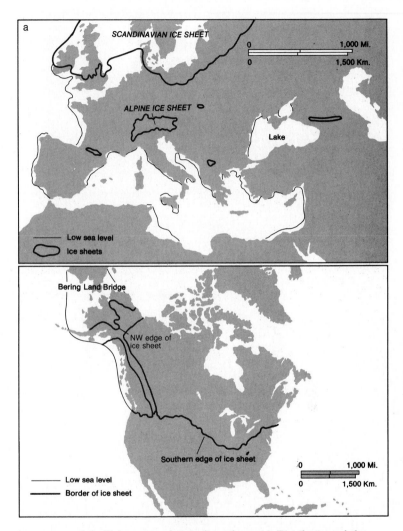

FIGURE 3.4 Pleistocene relative chronology. (a) Distribution of the
major ice sheets in Europe and North America during the last glaciation of the Pleistocene, and the extent of land exposed by low sea
levels; (b, following page) Provisional Ice Age chronology; (c, following page) Surroundings of a hunter-gatherer camp from northern
England, occupied about 10,000 years ago, reconstructed by pollen
analysis.

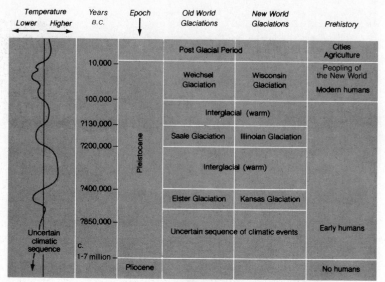

| Temperature Lower ← → Higher | Years B.C. | Epoch ↓ | Old World Glaciations | New World Glaciations | Prehistory |
|---|---|---|---|---|---|
| | | | Post Glacial Period | | Cities Agriculture |
| | 10,000 — | | Weichsel Glaciation | Wisconsin Glaciation | Peopling of the New World |
| | 100,000 — | | | | Modern humans |
| | ?130,000 — | Pleistocene | Interglacial (warm) | | |
| | ?200,000 — | | Saale Glaciation | Illinoian Glaciation | |
| | | | Interglacial (warm) | | |
| | ?400,000 — | | Elster Glaciation | Kansas Glaciation | |
| | ?850,000 — | | Uncertain sequence of climatic events | | Early humans |
| Uncertain climatic sequence ↓ | c. 1-7 million — | Pliocene | | | No humans |

b

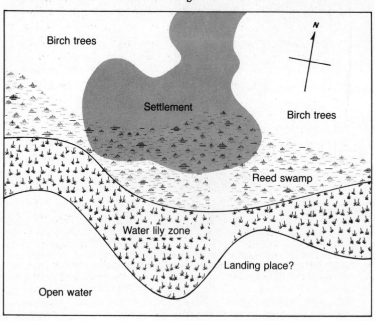

c

The framework of glaciations and warmer periods provides only a general chronology for prehistory. Relatively few prehistoric peoples lived on or very near the great ice sheets. But their campsites have been discovered on the shores of long-dried-up Pleistocene lakes that were later sealed by the movement of advancing ice sheets. The dried-up deposits of these lakes are rich in organic materials that provide a wealth of information on the environment at the time the site was occupied. Millions of tiny fossil pollen grains from the trees and undergrowth that once grew near the lake are preserved in the lake filling. These pollen grains are highly distinctive and readily identified, because each tree species, even each kind of grass, has a different form. By taking samples from the lake deposits, it is possible to reconstruct the vegetation around a Pleistocene lake by identifying and counting the fossil pollens.

This technique is **palynology**, the science of pollen analysis, about the only means of gaining an accurate picture of prehistoric environments in any detail. Pollen samples have shown how hunter-gatherers living in central Africa fifty thousand years ago were exploiting dense rainforests. In 10,000 B.C., present western Europe was covered with treeless arctic plains swept by icy winds. It has taken only a few thousand years for northern Europe to change from arctic climate to the temperate environment of today. Minute changes in vegetational cover accompanied these climatic shifts, changes that can be traced by studying pollens in the lake clays and muds in which many archaeological sites lie (Figure 3.4c), and each vegetation type can be assigned to a dated zone of post-Pleistocene time.

The Pleistocene also witnessed major changes in world sea levels. During glacial periods sea levels fell by several hundred feet, as water became locked up in huge ice sheets. When warmer climates returned, sea levels rose again. Some ancient high sea levels can be seen above the modern coastline. Sometimes prehistoric settlements are found on such high beaches, occupied when the oceans were more extensive than today. The geological date of the abandoned beach tells you the date of the site on it.

These sea-level changes radically altered world geography (Figure 3.4a). During periods of low sea level, people could

walk across the Bering Strait from Asia to North America,
and would hunt dry-shod over land that is now the English
Channel and the North Sea. Thousands of archaeological sites
are buried under the oceans, settlements that have the potential to tell us when people first entered North America.
Rising sea levels tended to isolate human populations, and,
like other climatic fluctuations, to encourage human adaptation to more varied environments than ever before. Without
question, the present diversity of humankind can, in part, be
attributed to the constant shifts in world climate over the past
two million years.

The relative chronology of the Pleistocene provides a general framework for the major events of prehistory. This framework becomes much more accurate after one hundred thousand years B.C., when many more sites are found near lakes
and other localities and pollen analysis can be used to study
vegetational and environmental changes.

## DATING IN YEARS (CHRONOMETRIC DATING)

People have tried everything to date the past in calendar
years. Today, a battery of such **chronometric**, or absolute,
dating methods are available to the archaeologist. Some are
reliable, well-tried techniques, such as tree-ring dating and
potassium argon dating. Others are most experimental, including amino acid racemization, obsidian hydration, and
thermoluminescence. We do not have the space to discuss all
these methods here, and so we shall confine ourselves to the
more widely used chronometric techniques. Fortunately,
these straddle most of prehistoric time (Figure 3.5). For the
more experimental methods, consult the "Further Reading"
section at the back of the book.

### Historical Records and Objects of Known Age

In the Near East, five thousand years of history are
recorded in government archives, in inscriptions, and on
thousands of clay tablets. As we saw in Chapter 1, archaeology provides us with a means for checking and expanding
historical records. But the lists of kings and genealogies in

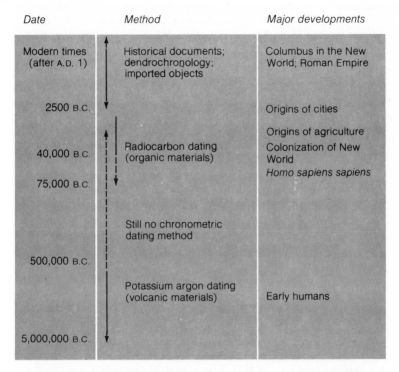

| Date | Method | Major developments |
|------|--------|--------------------|
| Modern times (after A.D. 1) | Historical documents; dendrochronology; imported objects | Columbus in the New World; Roman Empire |
| 2500 B.C. | | Origins of cities |
| 40,000 B.C. | Radiocarbon dating (organic materials) | Origins of agriculture<br>Colonization of New World<br>*Homo sapiens sapiens* |
| 75,000 B.C. | | |
| | Still no chronometric dating method | |
| 500,000 B.C. | | |
| | Potassium argon dating (volcanic materials) | Early humans |
| 5,000,000 B.C. | | |

FIGURE 3.5 Major chronological methods in prehistory. Experimental methods eliminated for clarity.

early Egyptian and Mesopotamian archives give us dates in years that go back to at least 3000 B.C. Recorded history starts in about 750 B.C. in the central Mediterranean, about 55 B.C. in Britain. The first historical records for the New World began with the Spanish Conquest, and parts of Africa entered "history" in A.D. 1890. Historical records cover but the very smallest fraction of the human experience.

Fortunately, the literate civilizations of three or four thousand years ago traded their products far and wide. The Egyptians traded fine ornaments to Crete, the Cretans sent wine and fine pottery to the Nile. When archaeologist Arthur Evans discovered the magnificent Minoan civilization of Crete in 1900, he dated the Palace of Knossos by means of Minoan pottery fragments that had been excavated in faraway Egypt, in levels whose precise historical date was known. Coins and other imports of known age can be used to date buildings or refuse pits in which they were dropped centuries earlier. A bewildering array of dated objects are used by archaeologists dealing with the recent periods of prehistory. These include glass bottles and beads, seals, imported Chinese porcelain, even military buttons. Each of these objects has the advantage that its age is known exactly.

### Tree-Ring Dating (Dendrochronology)

Everyone is familiar with the concentric growth rings that can be seen in the cross-section of a felled tree trunk. These rings, formed in most trees, are of special importance to archaeologists in areas like the American Southwest, where the seasonal weather changes markedly and growth is concentrated in a few months of the year. Normally trees produce two growth rings each year, which are formed by the cambium between the wood and the bark. Each year's growth forms a distinct ring that varies in thickness according to the tree's age and annual climatic variations. Weather variations in the Southwest tend to run in cycles of dry and wet years, which are reflected in patterns of thicker and thinner rings on the trees.

The tree-ring samples are taken with a borer from living or felled trees. The ring sequences from the borer are then compared to each other and to a master chronology of rings built up from many trees with overlapping sequences. The patterns of thick and thin rings for the new sequences are matched to the master sequence and are dated on the basis of their accurate fit to the master sequence. By using the California bristlecone pine, tree-ring experts have developed a master chronology over eight thousand years back into the past (Figure 3.6).

Tree-ring dating can be practiced on long-felled wood beams from Indian pueblos to date the buildings of which they are a part. Tree-ring experts have been able to develop an extremely accurate chronology for southwestern sites that extend back as long ago as 322 B.C. It was a difficult task, for they had to connect a prehistoric chronology from dozens of

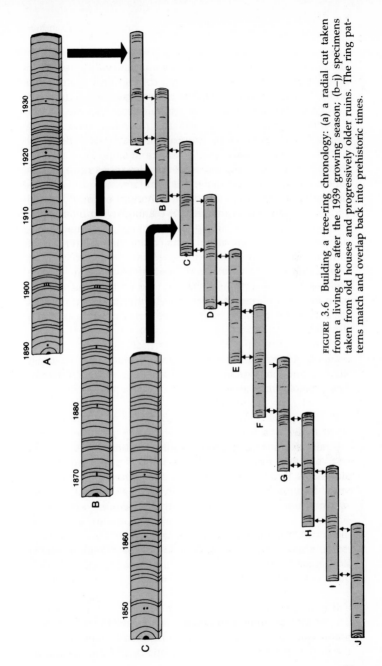

FIGURE 3.6 Building a tree-ring chronology: (a) a radial cut taken from a living tree after the 1939 growing season; (b–j) specimens taken from old houses and progressively older ruins. The ring patterns match and overlap back into prehistoric times.

ancient beams to a master tree-ring chronology connected to modern times obtained from living trees of known age. The dates of such famed southwestern sites as Mesa Verde and Pueblo Bonito are known to within a few years.

Dendrochronology has been used in other areas of the world as well—in Alaska and the American Southeast, and with great success in Greece, Ireland, and Germany. The bristlecone pine is to the Southwest as oaks are to Europe. European tree-ring experts have collected large numbers of tree-ring records from oaks that lived 150 years or so. By visual and statistical comparison they have linked living trees to ancient ones from bogs and prehistoric sites, and also farmhouse and church beams, providing a tree-ring sequence that goes back 7,272 years in northern Ireland and 6,000 years in Germany. Radiocarbon dates throughout Europe can now be calibrated to as early as 5,200 B.C. Dutch tree-ring experts have even tried dating the oak panels utilized by old masters as backing for their oil paintings as a way of authenticating paintings.

Unfortunately, tree-ring dating is limited to relatively recent settlements in restricted regions of markedly seasonal rainfall. But, as we shall see, dendrochronology is also useful for calibrating radiocarbon dates.

## Radiocarbon Dating

Radiocarbon dating, developed by physicists J. R. Arnold and W. F. Libby in 1949, is the best known of all chronometric methods. Cosmic radiation produces neutrons that enter the earth's atmosphere and react with nitrogen to produce the carbon isotope carbon 14 ($^{14}C$, or radiocarbon), which has eight rather than the usual six neutrons in its nucleus. With these additional neutrons, the nucleus is unstable and is subject to radioactive decay. Arnold and Libby calculated that it took 5,568 years for half of the $^{14}C$ in any sample to decay, the so-called half-life of $^{14}C$. (The half-life is now known to be 5,730 years).

Carbon 14 is believed to behave just like ordinary carbon ($^{12}C$) from a chemical standpoint. Together with $^{12}C$ it enters into the carbon dioxide of the atmosphere. Because living vegetation builds up its own organic matter by photosynthesis and by using atmospheric carbon dioxide, the ratio of $^{14}C$ to $^{12}C$ in living vegetation and the animals that eat it is equal to that in the atmosphere. As soon as an organism dies, no further radiocarbon is incorporated into it. The radiocarbon present in the dead organism will continue to disintegrate, so that after 5,730 years half the original amount will be left; after about 11,400 years, a quarter; and so on. Thus, measuring the amount of $^{14}C$ still present and emitting radiation in plant and animal remains enables us to determine the time that has elapsed since their death. By calculating the difference between the amount of $^{14}C$ originally present and that now present, and comparing the difference with the known rate of decay, we can compute the time elapsed in years. The amount of $^{14}C$ in a fresh sample emits particles at a rate of about fifteen particles per minute per gram of carbon. A sample with an emission rate of half that amount would be approximately 5,730 years old, the time needed for one-half the original radioactive material to disintegrate (the half-life of $^{14}C$).

Radiocarbon samples can be taken from many organic materials. About a handful of charcoal, burned bone, shell, hair, wood, or other organic substance is needed for the laboratory. This requisite means that few actual artifacts may be dated, for wood and other organic artifacts are rare. But charcoal from hearths is frequently used for dating. The samples themselves are collected with meticulous care from particular stratigraphic contexts so that an exact location, or a specific structure, is dated.

The laboratory converts the sample to gas and pumps it into a proportional counter. The beta particle emissions are measured, usually for twenty-four hours. The results of the count are then converted to an age determination. When a $^{14}C$ date comes from a laboratory, it bears a statistical plus or minus factor. For example, 3,600 $\pm$ 200 years (200 years represents one standard deviation) means that chances are two out of three that the correct date is between the span of 3,400 and 3,800. If we double the deviation, chances are nineteen out of twenty that the span 3,200 to 4,000 is correct. Radiocarbon dates should be recognized for what they are—statistical approximations.

The conventional radiocarbon method relies on measurements of a beta ray decay rate to date the sample. A number of laboratories are experimenting with an ultrasensitive mass spectrometer to count the individual carbon 14 atoms in a sample instead. This new, faster approach allows one to date much smaller samples, as small as a fragment of straw in a potsherd, and the results will be more accurate than those from a conventional reading. You can often date a tiny fragment of organic material from an actual artifact such as a potsherd, thereby dating the object itself.

The practical limits of radiocarbon dating with beta decay approaches are between 40,000 and 60,000 years. Researchers have tried detecting $^{14}$C atoms directly with a particle accelerator, a technique that would extend the limits of radiocarbon dating to as much as 100,000 years, although at present its limits, mainly because of contamination carried into soil by roots, are around 70,000 years.

When J. R. Arnold and W. F. Libby first developed radiocarbon dating, they compared their $^{14}$C readings with dates from objects of known age, such as ancient Egyptian boats. These tests enabled them to claim that radiocarbon dates were accurate enough for archaeologists' purposes. But just when archaeologists thought they had at last an accurate and reliable means for dating the past, some radiocarbon dates for dated tree rings of long-lived California bristlecone pines were published. They turned out to be consistently younger—for trees dating to before 1200 B.C.

It turned out that Libby had incorrectly assumed that the concentration of radiocarbon in the atmosphere has remained constant through time, so that prehistoric samples, when they were alive, would contain the same amount of radiocarbon as living things today. But, in fact, changes in the strength of the earth's magnetic field and alternations in solar activity have considerably varied the concentration of radiocarbon in the atmosphere and in living things.

Fortunately, however, it is possible to correct $^{14}$C dates back to about 4500 B.C. by calibrating them with tree-ring chronologies, for dendrochronology provides absolutely precise dates. Some idea of the changes in accuracy of $^{14}$C dating over the past six thousand years can be gathered from Figure 3.7. Calibration of dates earlier than 4500 B.C. is impossible because three-ring chronologies are lacking, but extreme accu-

| *Radiocarbon age* A.D./B.C. | *Calibrated age range* A.D./B.C. |
|---|---|
| A.D. 1500 | A.D. 1300 to 1515 |
| 1000 | 870 to 1230 |
| 500 | 265 to 640 |
| 1 | 420 to 5 B.C. |
| 500 B.C. | 820 to 400 |
| 1000 | 1530 to 905 |
| 1500 | 2345 to 1660 |
| 2000 | 2830 to 2305 |
| 2500 | 3505 to 2925 |
| 3000 | 3950 to 3640 |
| 3500 | 4545 to 3960 |
| 4000 | 5235 to 4575 |
| 4500 | 5705 to 5205 |
| 5000 | 6285 to 5445 |
| 5300 | 6585 to 5595 |
| before 5500 | Outside calibration range |

FIGURE 3.7   Widely agreed-upon calibrations for radiocarbon dates at 500-year intervals, from A.D. 1500 to 5300 B.C.

racy is less important for earlier periods anyway because time scales are less precise.

Despite its chronological and technical limitations, radiocarbon dating is of enormous significance to archaeology. Carbon 14 samples have dated some African hunter-gatherers to more than fifty thousand years ago and Paleo-Indian bison kills on the Great Plains to more than eight thousand years before the present, and they have provided chronologies for the origins of agriculture and civilization in the New World and the Old. Radiocarbon dates provide a means for developing a truly global chronology that can equate major events such as the origins of literate civilizations in such widely separated areas as China and Peru. The prehistory of the world from some forty thousand years ago up to historic times is dated almost entirely by the radiocarbon method. But most "finite" carbon 14 dates earlier than 40,000 years ago (and a lot of younger ones) are, in fact, minimum dates.

## Early Prehistory

Earlier than forty thousand years ago, we enter a long period of prehistory that is poorly dated. Some experimental dating methods such as *uranium thorium* and other uranium series methods are being worked out to fill this gap. But their archaeological applications are still very limited. Consult the references in "Further Reading" for a description of this and other experimental techniques.

The period between seventy-five thousand and five hundred thousand years ago was one of slow human cultural evolution, when *Homo sapiens* first appears in the archaeological record. At present, we have no idea exactly when, or how, modern human beings first evolved. Obviously, such information must await new dating methods and additional archaeological sites.

## Potassium Argon Dating

Some very early archaeological sites can be dated by a radioactive counting technique known as **potassium argon dating**. Geologists use this method to date rocks as early as four to five billion years ago and as recent as twenty thousand years before the present. Potassium (K) is one of the most abundant elements in the earth's crust and is present in nearly every mineral. In its natural form, potassium contains a small proportion of radioactive $^{40}K$ atoms. For every one hundred $^{40}K$ atoms that decay, 11 percent become argon 40, an inactive gas that can easily escape from its present material by diffusion when lava and other molten rocks are formed. As volcanic rocks form by crystallization, the concentration of argon 40 drops to almost nothing. but the decay of $^{40}$K continues, and 11 percent of every one hundred $^{40}$K atoms will become argon 40. It is possible therefore to measure the concentration of argon 40 that has accumulated since the rock formed, using a spectrometer.

Many archaeological sites, such as those at Olduvai Gorge, Tanzania, were formed during periods of intense volcanic activity. Dates have been determined for contemporary volcanic ashes, sometimes stratified above and below places where human tools and broken animal bones lie. Louis and Mary Leakey were able to get potassium argon dates for artifact and bone scatters at Olduvai, where early human fossils were found. The samples gave readings of about 1.75 million years.

Even earlier dates have come from sites at *Hadar* in Ethiopia and *Laetoli* in Tanzania, both in East Africa, where volcanic materials associated with early human fragments have been dated by potassium argon techniques to more than three million years ago. Stone flakes and chopping tools have come from *Koobi Fora* in northern Kenya, dated to about two million years.

Like carbon 14, potassium argon dates have a standard deviation, a few tens of thousands of years for early Pleistocene sites. On the other hand, because some of the world's most important early archaeological sites are found in volcanically active areas, we are fortunate in having at least a provisional chronology for the earliest chapters of human evolution, one far more accurate than the educated guesses of earlier generations. Potassium argon dating is getting ever more accurate, and one- to three-million-year-old East African dates now have standard deviations in the 20,000- to 50,000-year range. Recent improvements in dating techniques have both reduced statistical errors and extended the range of potassium argon dates into the past 100,000 years. Some 20,000-year-old dates with 5,000-year standard deviations have recently been processed. Perhaps, one day, potassium argon will take over where radiocarbon dating leaves off, between 40,000 and 75,000 years ago.

Archaeologists base their studies of time on precise stratigraphic excavations and records and on proven as well as experimental dating techniques. These data and analyses provide a provisional time scale for world prehistory. Potassium argon dates place human origins at least as early as four million years ago, the appearance of *Homo erectus* to about 1.5 million. Radiocarbon dates assign the earliest cave art of western Europe to earlier than 20,000 B.C., the origins of agriculture in the Near East to before 8000 B.C. We know that Mesopotamians were living in sizable city-states by 3200 B.C., the Olmec of Mexico flourishing before 1000 B.C. Tree-ring chronologies date Mesa Verde, Colorado, to A.D. 1150, and historical records and artifacts of known age enable us to cross-date hundreds of sites in Europe and the Americas within the recent millennia of prehistory. Hence, we have developed the first provisional chronology for a truly global world history and prehistory.

# 4

## SPACE

> After an artifact has been exposed, its position must .be recorded. This information is as significant as the artifact itself.
>
> ROBERT HEIZER, 1958

Space is another vital dimension of archaeological context—not the limitless space of the heavens, but a precisely defined location for every find made during an archaeological survey and excavation. Every archaeological find has an exact location in latitude, longitude, and depth measurement, which together identify any point in space absolutely and uniquely. When carrying out surface surveys or excavations, archaeologists use special methods to record the precise positions of artifacts, dwellings, and other finds. They tie in the position of each site to accurate survey maps, so that they can use the grid coordinates on the map to define the location precisely on the landscape. When investigating a site, they lay out recording grids made up of equal squares over the entire site, using the grids to record the exact position of each object on the surface or in the trenches (see Figure 6.1 for a site grid).

In Chapters 1 and 2, we saw that human behavior is patterned. Thus, it leaves patterns in the archaeological record that we can detect and interpret through the archaeologist's *spatial analysis*—the analysis of space.

Spatial location is indispensable to archaeologists because it enables them to establish the distances between objects or dwellings, or between entire settlements, or between settlements and key vegetational zones and landmarks. Such distances may be a few inches of level ground between a fine clay pot and the skeleton of its dead owner, or ten miles separating two seasonal camps. A team of fieldworkers may record the distance measurements between dozens of villages that traded luxury goods such as seashells over hundreds of miles. We can now distinguish two spatial considerations: the distribution of *artifacts within* a settlement, and the distribution of the *settlements themselves*. We return to this topic—settlement archaeology—in Chapter 9.

Context in space is closely tied to peoples' behavior. Archaeologists examine both an artifact itself and its association with other artifacts to gain insight into human behavior. The patterning of artifacts around an abandoned iron-smelting furnace or near the bones of a slaughtered bison is good evidence for specific human behavior. An isolated projectile head can tell you only that it was used as a weapon; but the patterning of projectile heads, scraping tools, and large boulders associated with a bison skeleton supplies a context in space that allows much more detailed inferences.

Collections of similar artifacts at contemporary sites within a reasonable geographic range are likely to have been made by people with the same culture. Such consistent patternings of artifact collections are the basis for classifying "archaeological cultures" and for studying how prehistoric cultures differ over space and through time (Chapter 7).

Space involves archaeologists in two directions of inquiry. The first is part of the process of describing one's finds, of determining the cultural origins of artifacts. This procedure of ordering is described more fully in Chapter 7, where we discuss some of the arbitrary analytical devices that archaeologists use. The second aspect of space involves studying specific activities—economic, religious, social, technological—within a human settlement. These patternings may reflect the activities of a person, a household, or an entire community.

## THE LAW OF ASSOCIATION

In the first analysis, context in space is based on **associations** between artifacts and other evidence of human behavior around them. Let us say you find a beer can opener in a plowed field. An expert on such artifacts—and they can be found—usually can date your opener to within a few years of its manufacture by going to manufacturers' files or U.S. Patent Office records. But your beer can opener was an isolated find. No other signs of human activity were discovered nearby. How could you infer, if you were not a twentieth-century American, that the artifact was used for opening a can? But had you found the can opener in association with a dozen punctured beer cans of similar age, you could then infer the general activity that took place, and you could draw some conclusions about the purposes for which the artifact in question was designed.

The law of association is based on the principle that an artifact is contemporary with the other objects found in the precise archaeological horizon in which it is found (Figure 4.1). The proof that humanity was far older than the six thousand years of Biblical chronology came when scientists found ancient stone axes in association with the bones of apparently older extinct animals. The mummy of Egyptian Pharaoh Tutankhamun was associated with an astonishing treasury of household possessions and ritual objects. This association provided unique information on Egyptian life in 1342 B.C.: the mummy alone would have been far less informative.

The law of association is of great importance when one is ordering artifacts in chronological sequences. Many prehistoric societies buried their dead with grave furniture—clay pots, bronze ornaments, seashells, or stone axes. In some cases, the objects buried with a corpse were obviously in use when their owner died. Occasionally, they may be prized heirlooms, passed down from generation to generation. Together they are an association of artifacts, a grave group that may be found duplicated in dozens of other contemporary graves. But later graves may be found to contain quite different furniture, vessels of a slightly altered form. Obviously some cultural changes had taken place. When dozens of burial groups are analyzed in this way, the associations and changing artifact styles may provide a basis for dividing the burials into different chronological groups (Figure 4.2).

Archaeological context can be both primary and secondary, as best illustrated with a burial mound. Someone important dies. His or her kinsfolk bury the important personage in a lavishly decorated grave covered with a large earthen mound, visible from a long distance. This is the **primary context** of

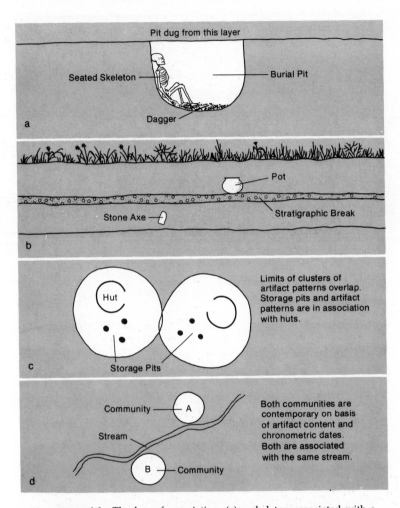

FIGURE 4.1 The law of association: (a) a skeleton associated with a dagger; (b) a pot and a stone axe, separated by a stratigraphic break, which are not in association; (c) two contemporary household clusters associated with each other; (d) an association of communities that are contemporary.

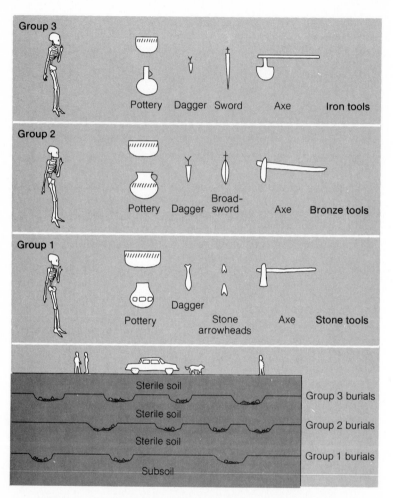

FIGURE 4.2 Burial groups divided into chronological groups by assessing associated artifacts. Group 1 burials contain no metal artifacts, but simply decorated shallow bowls that were made by all burial groups and show cultural continuity through time. The stone arrowheads of Group 1 are replaced by metal swords; daggers continue in use, made successively in stone, bronze, and iron. Continuity of artifacts is sufficient to place groups in sequence, using the law of association; this grouping was in fact confirmed by stratigraphic observation, shown at the bottom.

the burial mound. Many centuries later, some other people come along and bury a series of bodies in shallow pits dug into the higher levels of the mound. These are **secondary** burials, in a secondary context. If one of the later graves impinges upon the original grave pit, perhaps disturbing the body, archaeologists speak of primary and secondary burials.

## SUBASSEMBLAGES AND ASSEMBLAGES

Human behavior can be individual and totally unique, shared with other members of one's family or clan, or common to all members of a community. All these levels of cultural behavior should, theoretically, be reflected in artifact patterns and associations in the archaeological record. The iron projectile point found in the backbone of a British war casualty of A.D. 43 is clearly the consequence of one person's behavior, but that behavior is clearly related to the common cultural behavior of the warrior's society (Figure 4.3).

When more than one artifact is found in a patterned association that reflects the shared cultural behavior of a group of individuals, the artifacts are grouped in **subassemblages**, part of a toolkit that reflects a specific activity. A hunter uses a bow and arrows, which are carried in a quiver. An auto mechanic uses wrenches, screwdrivers, and gauges. Such subassemblages of artifacts are confined to particular individuals in society.

But what happens when quite dissimilar subassemblages of artifacts—let us say, hunting weapons and baskets and also digging sticks used in collecting plant foods—are found in a contemporary association? The artifacts together reflect in their patterning the shared activities of a total community and are known as an **assemblage**.

This shared behavior is reflected in the remains of houses—in the nonportable artifacts such as storage pits and hearths, inside and outside of them—and in community settlement patterns. Some early prehistoric Mexican villages consisted of groupings of square, thatched houses. Each house contained subassemblages that reflected the behavior of individual males and females, subassemblages inferred from artifact associations and patternings. The patterned household groups

FIGURE 4.3   An iron arrowhead embedded in the backbone of a British warrior killed during a battle with Roman soldiers at Maiden Castle, England, in A.D. 43.

in the village—that is, the associations of these subassemblages and the features associated with them—make up the larger assemblage of human behavior in space that constitutes the entire community (Figure 4.4).

## HOUSEHOLDS, COMMUNITIES, AND ACTIVITY AREAS

Archaeological sites can be classified in several ways. One way is by location: hilltop site, cave, rockshelter, hot-spring village, and so on. They can also be classified by the types of activity that took place in them. These activities are distinguished by patterning of artifacts and food remains within households and within the settlement. A kill site is identified from the presence of dismembered bison skeletons associated with scattered stone projectile heads and butchering tools. We find no houses, workshop areas, burials, or storage pits at a kill site; this is simply where the people cut up their prey.

Some sites defy such classification. The 1.75 million-year-old scatters of human artifacts and broken animal bones at Olduvai Gorge, Tanzania, lie in clusters of stone flakes and bones, with occasional gaps between them. Originally, Louis and Mary Leakey believed these were campsites, places where very early humans had dwelt for a few days while butchering game. But more recent research rejects this hypothesis, for close examination of the weathering on the bones shows that many had lain on the ancient land surface for between four and ten years. Most of them are limb bones, from a very diverse group of mammals, large and small. Many of the bones bear both stone tool cut marks and telltale knawings by carnivores such as hyenas. It may be that the accumulations of bones and stone tools marked places where early humans brought meat-rich bones they grabbed from lion and other predator kills. At such locations, they hastily cut off meat and marrow before abandoning the bones to prowling carnivores. The Olduvai "campsites" may, in fact, be bone caches used again and again over long periods.

Many later settlements contain the remains of individual houses, each occupied by a group of people who were members of a **household**. In these instances, we can examine the artifacts, hearths, and broken bones within, and around, the confines of one dwelling, and then compare the activities of individual households. Each house had its own storage areas, garbage pits, and so on, in much the same way as every suburban household has its own garage and garbage cans today (Figure 4.4). All the households in one settlement make up a **community**.

**Activity areas** are identified from characteristic artifact patternings preserved in the ground that reflect a set of tasks carried out by one or more members of a community (Figure 4.4). Activity areas can usually be identified by mapping a scatter of tools characteristic of a specialist activity such as

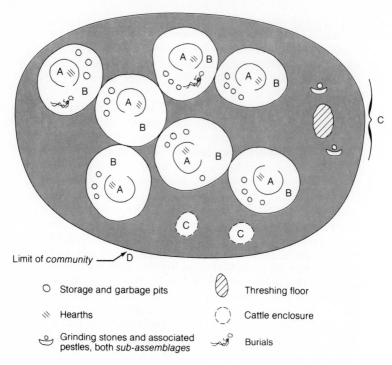

O   Storage and garbage pits

\\\\   Hearths

⌣   Grinding stones and associated
     pestles, both *sub-assemblages*

⌀   Threshing floor

( )   Cattle enclosure

⌣   Burials

FIGURE 4.4   A hypothetical prehistoric farming village: (a) houses; (b) household areas; (c) activity areas; (d) the community; (e) subassemblages. (An assemblage is all the artifacts from the site.)

bead making or stone-tool manufacture. Such activities usually took place within a limited area. Under favorable archaeological conditions, these artifact distributions can be used to compare differences in activities between separate households within a community. Some families may have been specialists in stone knife making, and others made shell beads or were expert metalworkers. The activity areas in these households may reflect such skills.

The behavior of an entire community is reflected in the distribution of houses and households, activity areas, and individual artifacts.

## CULTURE AREAS AND SETTLEMENT PATTERNS

But what happens when one considers several communities that share activities? Big-game hunting, long-distance trade, major religious ceremonies, and other such activities are often shared by entire cultures and societies. But these behavior patterns can be identified only by patterning in a number of assemblages at different sites. Such consistent patternings of assemblages represent an **archaeological culture**, the archaeological equivalent of a human society (Chapters 2 and 7). Archaeological cultures consist of material remains of human culture preserved at a specific space and time at several sites. A **culture area** is the geographic area over which the assemblages that make up a unique culture are defined in time and space. An example, from New Zealand, might be the Maori culture area, the region over which the characteristic toolkits of these remarkable people are found.

To see how behavior in a prehistoric society as a whole was patterned requires analyzing the ways in which communities and their associated assemblages are distributed on the landscape. Such distributions form **settlement patterns**, which we study with the aid of distribution maps. Many factors interact to determine settlement paterns. These include the natural environment with its seasonal changes, the distribution of plant and animal food resources, peoples' economic practices, and technological skills. Learned cultural patterns and established relationships between different peoples have a compelling influence on settlement patterns in some societies.

The !Kung San hunter-gatherers of the Kalahari Desert live in small camps of a few families by small water holes (Figure 4.5).[1] They move campsites through the year as water supplies become more plentiful or scarcer and vegetable foods within walking distance of each home base are exhausted. Each group of families has a regular set of localities they camp at each year. The amount of time they spend at each varies. The resources of their hunting and gathering territory can support only a few people per square mile, and so the dif-

---

[1] The ! symbol denotes a click sound made with the tongue.

FIGURE 4.5   A San nuclear family group; a few families live together
in campsites near water holes, moving as water supplies increase or
diminish.

ferent camps are widely dispersed over the landscape. Because the San have no large containers for carrying water or
great quantities of food, they return home most nights, having ventured out only as far as they can walk, forage com-
fortably, and return in daylight. Thus, the !Kung settlement
pattern of widely dispersed campsites by water holes results
from many interlinked variables.

A settlement pattern and a culture area do not necessarily
coincide. The settlement patterns of the Maya in Mesoamerica
consisted of large ceremonial centers with elaborate pyramids, temples, plazas, and houses, surrounded by, and
linked with, secondary ceremonial centers, which in turn
were related to a hierarchy of lesser settlements. But this
Maya settlement pattern is merely one part of the Maya cultural system and culture area, the larger area through which

characteristic Maya artifact assemblages can be recognized in time and space.

The concepts of culture, time, and space in archaeology are absolutely inseparable. A minimal definition of archaeology is the study of the interrelations between the form of artifacts found in a site, and their date and spatial location. All scientific archaeology, whether survey, excavation, laboratory analysis, or sophisticated theoretical argument encompassing thousands of artifacts, is based on the two critical concepts—time and space—which make up archaeological context.

# 5

# PRESERVATION
# AND SURVEY

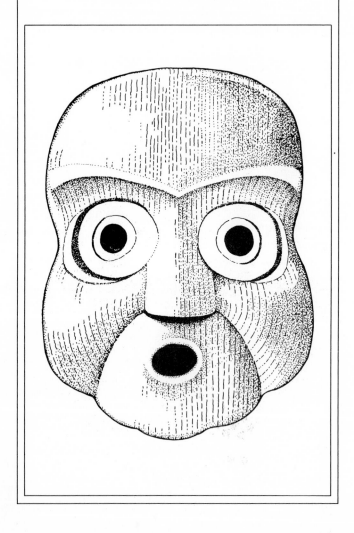

> Antiquities are history defaced, or some remnants
> of history which have casually escaped the ship-
> wreck of time.
>
> FRANCIS BACON, 1605

## PRESERVATION

Archaeologists are thought to live in a suspenseful world of rich burials and magnificent treasure houses crammed with gold and dazzling jewels. Object by object, the catalog unfolds as our heroes uncover wonder after new wonder. With breathless suspense, they lift the gilded sarcophagus from the pharaoh's coffin and peer into its mysterious interior. The long-dead king's bandaged corpse stares up at the excited archaeologists. Then, as they watch, the mummy "crumbles to dust on exposure to the outside air." The past has returned to its mysterious oblivion and the archaeologists see fame and fortune slip from their tantalized grasp. Such, we are told, are the fortunes of archaeology.

It is an uncomfortable fact of life that many archaeological finds do crumble to dust once they are exposed to the atmosphere or removed from the environment that may have protected them intact for thousands of years. The preservation of delicate finds such as mummies, textiles, and wood tools is a highly technical and time-consuming business. It is a tragedy that so many spectacular archaeological finds were made, in Egypt, the American West, and elsewhere, before the technology of preservation was even partially developed.

The preservation of such fragile, organic archaeological remains as bone, leather, skin, textiles, and wood depends on

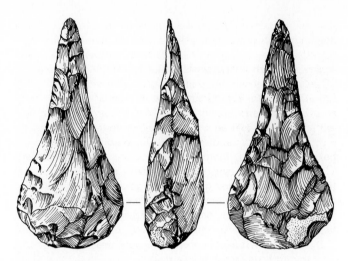

FIGURE 5.1 Three views of an *Acheulian* stone axe from Swanscombe on the River Thames, England.

their physical environment. Soil and climatic conditions very strongly influence archaeological materials. The inorganic artifacts—stone, baked clay pots, mud bricks, gold, copper, and bronze—preserve best. Much of the surviving archaeological record consists of such durable materials in the form of human tools (Figure 5.1).

Prehistoric peoples used many organic substances, materials that survive at relatively few locations. Bone and antler were commonly used by early hunter-gatherers, especially in Europe some fifteen thousand years ago. The desert peoples of western North America relied heavily on plant fibers and baskets for their material culture. Both hard and soft woods were used for digging sticks, bows and arrows, and other tools and weapons. Cotton textiles were much prized in coastal Peru two thousand years ago. Nearly every human society collected wild vegetable foods for part of their livelihood. These and traces of broken animal bones and other food remains are sometimes found when preservation conditions are favorable.

What are the most favorable conditions for preservation of

archaeological finds? The fantastically rich tomb of the Egyptian pharaoh Tutankhamun, who died in 1342 B.C., yielded incredible finds, including the pharaoh's personal wooden furniture, much of his clothing, and the perishable ritual objects that accompanied the dead king to the next world (see Figure 2.4, p. 34.). Tutankhamun's tomb is the only pharaoh's burial ever to be discovered intact, undisturbed by tomb robbers. The richness of the grave furniture came as a complete surprise. And the survival of the funeral bouquets, which showed that the king had died in the spring, was certainly exceptional. Dry conditions like those of the Nile Valley have led to remarkable discoveries in the desert western United States as well, where caves in Utah and Nevada have yielded not only sandals, bows and arrows, and other wood and fiber objects, but thousands of seeds, and even human droppings (coprolites or feces), which can be analyzed to give information on prehistoric diet (Chapter 8).

Waterlogged, flooded sites too aid preservation. They can seal off organic finds in an oxygen-free atmosphere. Danish archaeologists have found prehistoric dugout canoes deep in ancient peat bogs, along with leather clothing, traps, and wood spears. Their most famous finds are the corpses of sacrificial victims buried in the bogs more than two thousand years ago. We can gaze on the serene countenance of Tollund man. His corpse is in such excellent condition that we know he did not eat for at least twenty-four hours before his death, and that his last meal was a porridge of barley and wild grasses (Figure 5.2).

Richard Daugherty has gained unusual insights into prehistoric whale hunting on the northwest coast of America by digging a Makah Indian village at Ozette, Washington, long buried by sudden mudslides. The wet mud crushed cedar plank houses by the ocean, sealing their contents from the destructive effects of the atmosphere. The Ozette village was occupied for more than two thousand years, right into the twentieth century. Daugherty's buried houses provided a wealth of information about Makah Indian life and artistic traditions of centuries ago. The thick mud preserved walls and beams, sleeping benches, and fine mats. Wood fish hooks, seal-oil bowls, cedar storage boxes, and whaling harpoons were uncovered by fine water jets from pressure hoses

FIGURE 5.2 Tollund man, a remarkably well-preserved corpse discovered in the peat bogs of Denmark.

FIGURE 5.3   Richard Daugherty examines a whale fin carved of cedar wood, found at the Ozette site, and inlaid with 700 sea otter teeth. The teeth at the base are set in the design of a mythical bird with a whale in its talons.

washing mud from soft wood. The most remarkable find of all was a whale fin carved of red cedar and inlaid with sea otter teeth, a unique ritual object without parallel in North America (Figure 5.3). Fortunate is the archaeologist who finds a site with conditions as good as those at Ozette. They are very much the exception rather than the rule.

Arctic cold has frozen the past. When Russian archaeologist Sergei Rudenko excavated the burial mounds of *Pazyryk* in Siberia, he found long-dead prehistoric horsemen, accompanied by their horses and carts. The sites had literally been refrigerated, and so Rudenko recovered not only organic materials, but such fragile objects as Persian rugs, leather horse trappings, even the tattooed skin of the horsemen.

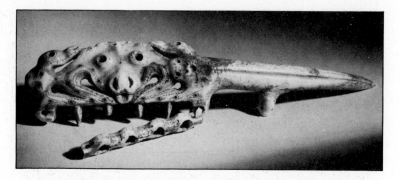

FIGURE 5.4   A walrus ivory object of unknown use of the *Ipiutak* culture, *ca*. 1,500 years old, 26 centimeters long. The Arctic artistic traditions of North America have been dated by means of changing motifs and styles on bones and ivory artifacts.

Eskimo archaeology has benefited greatly from frozen soils, for beautiful ivory and bone artifacts have survived almost intact for thousands of years. The Arctic artistic traditions of the north have been dated back, by means of changing motifs and styles of harpoons, thousands of years before the present (Figure 5.4).

But most archaeological sites yield only a fraction of the organic materials buried in them. The fortunate archaeologist may recover not only manufactured tools but some food remains as well—animal bones or a handful of shells, seeds, or other vegetable remnants. Obviously the picture one obtains of the inhabitants at such a site is incomplete compared with that from Ozette, Pazyryk, and elsewhere. And, because of archaeologists' constant preoccupation with ancient environments and prehistoric lifeways, sites with exceptional preservation conditions are obviously of paramount importance.

## FINDING ARCHAEOLOGICAL SITES

How do you know where to dig? How do you find sites or conduct an archaeological survey? Many people are amazed at how archaeologists seem to have an uncanny ability to choose the place for their excavations. Yet, most often they have merely used common sense or well-tried survey techniques to locate their site.

Finding archaeological sites involves far more than merely locating a prehistoric settlement to dig. Some archaeological sites are so conspicuous that people have always known of their existence. The pyramids of Giza in Egypt have withstood the onslaught of tourists, treasure hunters, and quarrymen for thousands of years. The Pyramid of the Sun at Teotihuacán, Mexico, is another easily visible archaeological site (see Figure 9.1). The eastern United States is dotted with hundreds of burial mounds and earthworks, which are easily distinguished from the surrounding countryside. Sites of this type are obviously simple to identify, and have been known for centuries.

Most archaeological sites are far less conspicuous. They may consist of little more than a scatter of pottery fragments or a few stone tools lying on the surface of the ground. Other settlements may be buried under several feet of soil, leaving few surface traces except when exposed by moving water, wind erosion, or burrowing animals. Cemeteries may be marked by piles of stones, and the deep accumulations of occupation deposits at the mouths of rock shelters or caves or the huge piles of abandoned shells left by shellfish collectors are more readily located. Finding archaeological sites depends on locating such telltale traces of human settlement. Once the sites have been found, they have to be recorded, and surface collections must be made at each locality to assemble a general impression of the activities of the people who lived there.

## DELIBERATE ARCHAEOLOGICAL SURVEY

An **archaeological survey** can vary from searching a city lot during an afternoon for traces of historical structures, to a large-scale survey of an entire river basin or drainage area, over several years. In all cases, the theoretical ideal is easily stated: to record all traces of ancient settlement in the area. But this ideal is impossible to achieve. Many sites leave no traces above the ground. And no survey, however thorough and however sophisticated its remote sensing devices, will ever achieve the impossible dream of total coverage. *The key to effective archaeological survey actually lies in carefully designing the research before one sets out in the field, and in using techniques to estimate the probable density of archaeological sites in the region.*

Archaeological surveys are most effective in terrain where the vegetation is burned off or sparse enough for archaeologists to be able to see the ground. In lush vegetation areas like that of the American South, only the most conspicuous earthworks will show up. And, of course, thousands of sites are buried under housing developments, parking lots, and artificial lakes that have radically altered the landscape in many places.

A great deal depends on the intensity of the survey in the field. The most effective surveys are carried out on foot, when the archaeologist can locate the traces of artifacts, the gray organic soil eroding from a long-abandoned settlement, and the subtle colors of rich vegetation that reveal long-buried houses. Plowed fields may display revealing traces of ash, artifacts, or hut foundations. Scatters of broken bones, stone implements, potsherds, or other traces of prehistoric occupation are easily located in such furrowed soil. *Observation is the key to finding archaeological sites and to studying the subtle relationships between prehistoric settlements and the landscape on which they flourished.*

Archaeologists have numerous inconspicuous signs to guide them. Gray soil from a rodent burrow, a handful of humanly fractured stones in the walls of a desert arroyo, a blurred mark in a plowed field, a potsherd—these are the signs they seek. And often, information on possible sites is provided by knowledgeable local inhabitants.

There is far more to archaeological survey than merely walking the countryside, however. Such surveys can be of varying intensity. The least intensive survey is the most common, the investigator examining only conspicuous and accessible sites, those of great size and considerable fame. Heinrich Schliemann followed just this procedure when he discovered the site of ancient Troy at Hissarlik in Turkey in the 1870s. John Lloyd Stephens and Frederick Catherwood did the same thing when they visited Uxmal, Palenque, and other Maya sites in Mesoamerica in the early 1840s. Such superficial surveys barely scratch the archaeological surface.

A more intensive survey involves collecting as much information about as many sites as possible from local informants and landowners. Again, the sites located by this means are the larger and more conspicuous ones, and the survey is necessarily incomplete. But this approach is widely used throughout the world, especially in areas where archaeologists have never worked before.

Many more discoveries will be made if the archaeologists undertake a highly systematic survey of a relatively limited area. This type of survey involves not only comprehensive inquiries among local landowners, but actual systematic checking of the site reports on the ground. The footwork resulting from the checking of local reports may lead to more discoveries. But, again, the picture may be very incomplete, for the survey deals with known sites and does not cover the area systematically from one end to the other or establish the proportions of each type of site known to exist in the region.

The most intensive surveys have a party of archaeologists covering a whole area by walking all over it, often in straight lines, with a set distance between the fieldworkers. Such surveys are usually based on carefully formulated research designs. The investigators are careful to check that their site distributions reflect actual prehistoric settlement patterns rather than where archaeologists walked. Between 1979 and 1981, a group of archaeologists headed by Garth Sampson surveyed several thousand square miles of the Seacow River Valley in South Africa, looking for late Stone Age hunting and gathering activity. Sampson noticed that most sites lay on low hills and ridges in dense clusters. Did these clusters reflect a concentration of archaeologists, or prehistoric reality?

The Sampson team developed a comprehensive survey plan that assessed every part of the study area with aerial photographs, maps, and on the ground. They then decided which areas they would eliminate on the grounds that they were unlikely to yield many sites. An 85 square kilometer area was randomly selected and covered by a grid of 2.47 acre (1 hectare) squares. Then 66.75 percent of the test area was searched on foot, the remainder, mainly steep slopes and flats, was not visited. Only 6.1 percent of the searched

squares yielded sites, suggesting that the observed site clusters were real ones, occupied areas surrounded by zones
where no camps or other activity areas were sited. Sampson
was able to show that 64 percent of the sites in the test area
occurred on 30 percent of the land, all of it within 0.62 mile
(1 km) of a dependable water hole. Statistically, this distribution is highly significant. This survey provided valuable
information on ancient hunting and settlement practices.

Clearly, most archaeological surveys can record only a sample of the sites in the survey area, even if the declared objective is to plot the position of every prehistoric settlement.
Such has been the purpose of an ambitious survey of the
Basin of Mexico, home of the Teotihuacán and Aztec civilizations of the past two thousand years. The investigators
have managed to chronicle the changing settlement patterns
in the Basin since long before Teotihuacán rose to prominence
after A.D. 100 right up to the Spanish conquest and beyond.
But they would be the first to admit that they have recovered
only a fraction of the Basin's sites. For a start, most of the
Aztec capital, Tenochtitlán, and its outlying suburbs lie under
the foundations of Mexico City.

In the early days, archaeologists concentrated on conspicuous, easily found sites. Now, with so many sites endangered
by all kinds of industrial development, they hurry to locate
as many prehistoric locations as possible. Often, a survey is
designed to make an inventory of an archaeological resource
base in a specific area. When an area is to be deep-plowed
or covered with houses, the burden of proof that archaeological sites do or do not exist in the endangered zone is the
responsibility of the archaeologists. Often, time is short and
funds are very limited. The only way the archaeologists can
estimate the extent of the site resource base is to survey selected areas in great detail. Those areas are determined by
careful research design and knowledge of the variables that
affect site location. The density and distribution of sites in
these areas are then used as a basis for generalizing from the
sample survey areas to larger regions. The reliability of these
vital generalizations is tested by routine statistical procedures.
This approach to archaeological survey, often called predic-
tive modeling, is still relatively new, and is somewhat controversial. It is assuming weight as a weapon to counter the

wholesale destruction of archaeological sites by industrial activity. Archaeologists cannot stop the destruction of every threatened site. The best they can hope for is a chance to make decisions on which sites in the archaeological resource base are to be preserved, which excavated before destruction, and which are to be destroyed in the name of progress.

All archaeologists have the responsibility for managing the priceless resource base of sites that is our legacy from the past. More and more archaeology in North America results from efforts to conserve sites and to manage a diminishing resource base. This activity is known as **cultural resource management**, and involves not only finding sites and investigating them, but making decisions about their fate as well—managing the past.

Obviously, accurate maps and record keeping are essential to any archaeological survey. And locating sites is pointless without making some attempt to establish their probable content and age. No one has the resources to excavate every site located in a survey, but, in areas where nothing is known, a representative surface collection from all located sites is essential. The artifacts on the surface of a site can give an idea of the occupations and activities that took place there. Surface collections can give little more than a general impression of site contents, for the effects of pot hunting, erosion and weathering, and burrowing animals can decimate surface scatters of artifacts. The site may have been occupied more than once, or may have been the location of some specialist activities such as hunting or stone tool making. In such sites, every object on the surface must be collected according to a carefully formulated sampling design. But even then, surface collection is no substitute for excavation.

## AERIAL PHOTOGRAPHY

The building of today's inventories of archaeological sites would never have been possible without aerial survey techniques. Aerial photography gives an overhead view of the past. Sites can be photographed from many directions, at different times of day, and at various seasons. Numerous sites that left almost no surface traces on the ground have been discovered by analyzing air photographs. Many earthworks and other complex structures have been leveled by plows or erosion, but their original layout shows up clearly from the air (Figure 5.5). The rising or setting sun can make large shadows emphasizing the relief of almost-vanished banks or ditches; the features of the site stand out in oblique light. Such phenomena are sometimes called "shadow sites."

In some areas, it is possible to detect differences in soil color and in the richness of crop growth on a particular soil. Such marks are hard to detect on the surface but often show up clearly from the air. The growth and color of a crop are greatly determined by the amount of moisture the plant can derive from the soil and subsoil. If the soil depth has been increased by digging features such as pits and ditches, later filled in, or because additional earth has been heaped up to form artificial banks or mounds, the crops growing over such abandoned structures are high and well nourished. The opposite is also true, where soil has been removed and the infertile soil is near the surface, or where impenetrable surfaces such as paved streets are below ground level and the crops grow less thickly. Thus, a dark crop mark can be taken for a ditch or pit, and a lighter line will define a more substantial structure.

Much of the world has been photographed from twenty-four thousand feet by military photographers. Such coverage has been put to use by archaeologists to survey remote areas such as the Virú Valley in Peru, where a team of archaeologists led by Gordon Willey plotted 315 sites on a master map of the valley. Many of the sites were stone buildings or agricultural terraces, others were refuse mounds that appeared as low hillocks on the photographs. By using aerial surveys, Willey saved days of survey time, for he was able to pinpoint many sites before going out in the field. When the settlements were visited, the fascinating story of shifting settlement patterns in Virú over thousands of years was made visible by a combination of foot survey and air photography.

## REMOTE SENSING

Aerial remote-sensing devices of many types have become available in recent years to complement the valuable results

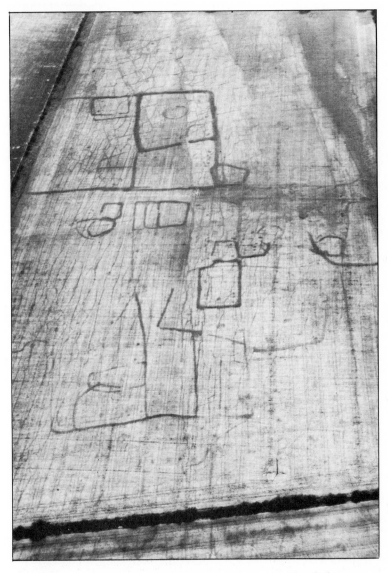

FIGURE 5.5  A long-lost archaeological site revealed by dark crop marks.

of black and white photography. Infrared film, which has three layers sensitized to green, red, and infrared, detects reflected solar radiation at the near end of the electromagnetic spectrum, some of which is invisible to the naked eye. The different reflections from cultural and natural features are translated by the film into distinctive "false" colors. Vigorous grass growth on river plains shows up in bright red. Such red patterns have been used in the American Southwest to track shallow, subsurface water sources where springs were used by prehistoric peoples. The infrared data could lead the archaeologist to likely areas for previously undetected hunting camps and villages.

In some areas, exuberant vegetation hampers archaeological surveys, especially in the Maya lowlands. For years, archaeologists have wondered how the Maya civilization managed to feed itself and have puzzled over the incompletely known distribution of its cities and ceremonial centers. Originally they believed that the Maya population was supported by "slash-and-burn" cultivation, a system still used today, in which people burn off and clear the forests, then cultivate the land for three or four years before leaving it fallow and moving on to new virgin plots. But so many sites are now known that we can be certain that the population was far larger than such a simple agricultural system could handle. Some surveys and excavations suggested that the Maya may have drained swamps and used irrigated lands, but no large-scale fieldwork was possible in the hot and densely overgrown rainforest.

A group of archaeologists, looking for a sensor system that would penetrate the dense forest cover of the area and see through silt and root cover to map ancient roads, causeways, and other humanly made structures invisible on the surface, discovered an unexpected archaeological payoff in the imaging radar developed by NASA for spaceborne lunar sounders and in synthetic aperture radar. (The radar chosen for the Maya experiment was, in fact, developed for imaging the surface of the planet Venus.) Flights were made over the Maya lowlands in 1978 and 1980, using black and white and color infrared film to search for indications of archaeological sites and ancient landscape modifications. When the features discovered were plotted onto topographic maps, they revealed not only shadows from large mounds and buildings, but irregular grids of gray lines within swampy areas near known major sites. These lines were found to form ladder-and-lattice as well as curvilinear patterns, which very closely matched conventional aerial views of known canal systems from the Valley of Mexico and the lowlands. The investigators believe that further radar surveys will reveal that the Maya grew large food surpluses using large-scale swamp agriculture, developing field systems that are nearly invisible on the ground today. The method is still experimental, however.

Aerial sensor imagery using aircraft, satellites, and even manned spacecraft, is prohibitively expensive and still rarely used in archaeology. The best-known source of aircraft-borne sensor imagery is Sideways-Looking Airborne Radar (SLAR). This radar system senses the terrain on either side of an aircraft's track, with the instrumentation tracking the pulse lines in the form of images, whether or not clouds obscure the ground. This approach has been used not only for tracing Maya agricultural systems, but in attempts to detect buildings under dense rainforest canopy. Satellite sensor imagery is used for both military and environmental monitoring. The best-known satellites are the LANDSAT series, which scan the earth with readers that detect the intensity of reflected light and infrared radiation from the earth's surface. These data are converted electronically into photographic images and mosaic maps, normally at a scale of about 1:1,000,000, too imprecise except for the most general of archaeological surveys. But Landsat imagery has great potential for studying present and past environments, as a backdrop for more detailed aerial and ground reconnaissance.

Aircraft and satellite scanning imagery will be more commonly used in archaeology, but the high cost will probably limit their application for the foreseeable future.

Fortunately, some geophysical prospecting tools carry more moderate cost. They are of great use when a site has been located and the archaeologist wants to find buried subsurface features such as stone walls. A resistivity survey meter is sometimes used to measure the variations in the resistance (resistivity) of the ground to electric current. Stone walls or hard pavement retain less dampness than a deep pit filled with soft earth or a silted-up ditch. These differences can be measured accurately with a resistivity meter, which records the resistivity "contours" across a grid of squares laid out on the site. On well-drained soils, resistivity surveys can locate their drier areas where buried ditches and walls lie.

Most people are familiar with the mine detector, a device used by many beachcombers and treasure hunters to search for loot. Although the companies selling such devices often promote them as a means for finding wealth in the ground, archaeologists have turned such electromagnetic detection devices to good use to find iron objects, fired clay furnaces, hearths, and pottery kilns. A proton magnetometer is used to measure the differences between the remanent magnetism of undisturbed soil and that of nearby subsurface features such as pottery kilns that have been heated in the past. The heated features retain a weak magnetism different from that of the earth's magnetic field. Magnetic detecting has been used very successfully to record pits, walls, and other features in the middle of large fortified towns and in ceremonial centers where total excavation of a site is clearly uneconomic.

## ACCIDENTAL DISCOVERIES

Whole chapters of the past have been retrieved by accidental discoveries of sites, spectacular artifacts, or skeletons. Dramatic finds have resulted from despoiling of the environment. Deep plowing and freeway and dam construction have led to the uncovering—and damaging—of priceless sites. When Mexico City's Metro (subway) was tunneled under the modern city, the twenty-eight miles of tunnels yielded a wealth of archaeological material. Mexico City is built on the site of the Aztec city of Tenochtitlán, overthrown by Hernando Cortés in 1521. Little remains of the Aztec city on the surface today. But the contractors for the Metro recovered forty tons of pottery, 380 burials, and even a small temple dedicated to the wind god Ehecatl-Quetzalcoatl. The temple is now preserved on its original site as part of the Piño Suarez station of the Metro system. All the tunneling operations were under the supervision of expert archaeologists, who were empowered to halt construction whenever an archaeological find was made.

Even more dramatic was the accidental rediscovery of the great Templo Mayor in the heart of Mexico City. Modern construction activity revealed the most sacred shrine of Aztec Tenochtitlán, the temples of the gods Huitzilopochtli and Tlaloc. Mexican archaeologist Eduardo Matos Moctezuma's excavations subsequently unearthed at least five successive temples and many rebuildings going back to as early as A.D. 1390, if not earlier. The temple visited by Spanish conquistador Hernando Cortés had 114 steps, with a drum so loud it could be heard six miles away. The conquistadors pulled it down to build a Catholic cathedral nearby. The abandoned shrines were forgotten until the 1970s.

The fields of the Western world have yielded many caches of buried weapons, coins, smith's tools, and sacrificial objects, valued treasures that were buried in times of stress by their owners. For whatever reason, the owners never returned to recover their valuables. Thousands of years later, a farmer comes across the hoard and, if a responsible citizen, reports the find to archaeological authorities. If not, yet another valuable fragment of the past is lost to science.

Nature itself sometimes uncovers sites for us, which are then located by a sharp-eyed archaeologist looking for natural exposures of likely geological strata. Olduvai Gorge is a great gash in the Serengeti Plains of northern Tanzania. An ancient earthquake opened a deep gorge, exposing hundreds of feet of lake bed that had been buried long before. It is these buried lake deposits that have yielded early tool and bone concentrations dating to at least 1.75 million years ago. They would never have been found without the assistance of an earthquake and subsequent erosion. The Olduvai area is but one of many examples from all over the world where nature has revealed the incredible bounty of the past.

The archaeologist of today cares not only about the discovery of sites but their preservation and management as well. The archaeological record consists of thousands of sites that can never be replaced. In a sense, all archaeologists are managers of this archive. More and more archaeological surveys are conducted in advance of bulldozers and major construction projects. Often archaeologists have to estimate how many sites in an area remain undiscovered after their survey, and then recommend to federal or state agencies what measures, if any, should be taken to minimize the effects of a major land-use project on the archaeological resources they have discovered. This type of archaeological survey is still in its infancy. It results from recent local, state, and federal legislation recognizing that archaeological sites are an important natural resource. And the stakes are high. Without adequate surveys and efforts at resource management, it is safe to say that the future of archaeology in some parts of the world, especially North America and western Europe, would be in grave doubt. There would simply be nothing left for science.

# 6

# EXCAVATION

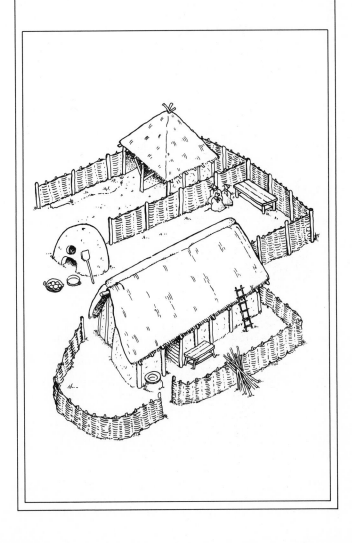

A mere hole in the ground, which of all sights is perhaps the least vivid and dramatic, is enough to grip their attention for hours at a time.

P. G. WODEHOUSE, 1919

Modern archaeological excavation is a precise and demanding science, which has the objective of recording archaeological sites and their contents in exact detail. In this chapter we describe some of the basic principles of excavation and some of the many excavation problems that archaeologists can encounter in the field. Realize, though, that each site presents distinctive problems and requires modification of the basic principles enumerated below.

## EXCAVATION

The first principle of excavation is that digging is destruction. The archaeological deposits so carefully examined during a dig are destroyed forever. Site contents are removed to a laboratory, permanently divorced from their context in time and space in the ground. Here is a radical difference from other disciplines. A chemist can readily recreate the conditions of a basic experiment. The biographer can return to the archives to reevaluate the complex events in a politician's life. But an archaeologist's archives are destroyed during the dig. All that remains from an excavation are the finds from the trenches, the unexcavated portions of the site, and the photographs, notes, and drawings that record the excavator's observations for posterity. One of the tragedies of archaeology is that much of the available archaeological data have been excavated under far from scientific conditions. Our archives of information are uneven at best.

The treasure hunter destroys a site in search of valuable finds, and keeps no records. Archaeologists destroy sites as well, but with a difference. They create archives of archaeological information that document contexts for the objects they take back to the laboratory with them. Although they have destroyed the site forever, they have created a data bank of information in its place, the only archive their successors will be able to consult to check their results. Archaeologists have serious responsibilities: for recording and interpreting the significance of the layers, houses, food remains, and artifacts in their sites, and for publishing the results for posterity. Without accurate records and meaningful publication of results of an excavation is useless. Regrettably, far too many interesting and important excavations have never been recorded in print and the results are lost forever.

A generation ago, archaeologists' first inclination was to dig sites to solve problems. Nowadays, there is increased awareness that excavation destroys irreplaceable evidence of the past, and they dig only when they have to. Anyone who digs without experience of record keeping and all the other processes of serious excavation is committing vandalism of an unforgivable kind. No treasure hunting or pot collecting, please!

## RESEARCH DESIGN

It follows that any archaeological excavation must be conducted from a sound research design that is intended to solve specific problems. The research design is created in the first stages of an investigation before a trench has been started or the crew assembled. It consists of a set of hypotheses to be tested against the data from the excavations. The research design is a flexible, ever-changing plan, modified as hypotheses are tested, proved wrong, validated, or refined as a result of the fieldwork.

The end products of even a month's excavation on a moderately productive site are boxes upon boxes of potsherds, stone tools, bones, and other finds that have to be cleaned, sorted, marked, and studied once the excavation is complete. Rolls of drawings completed in the field hold valuable stratigraphical information. So also do slides, photographs, and hundreds of pages of field notes compiled by the director of the excavation as the long days of digging continue. Radiocarbon and soil samples are collected for analysis. Freshwater shells and charcoal fragments are packed ready for shipment to specialist investigators. One expert excavator told me that it took a minimum of six months to analyze the finds from a month's excavation. The dozens of boxes and hundreds of notebook pages contain a large array of interconnected facts that have to be joined together to reconstruct the site in its original state. The research design is constantly reevaluated to determine the future course of the dig. The days when a site was dug simply because it "looked good" are long gone.

Illinois archaeologists Stuart Struever and James Brown spent many field seasons excavating the Koster site in the lower Illinois River Valley. Here, at least twelve human occupations are represented at one site, the earliest of which dates to before 5100 B.C. Koster is a deep site, probably abandoned before A.D. 1000 after generations of Indians had settled at this favorable locality. It offered Brown and Struever a unique opportunity to examine the changing cultures of the inhabitants over more than six thousand years. But the organizational problems were enormous. Koster is more than thirty feet deep, with each of the twelve cultural horizons separated from its neighbor by zones of sterile soil. Brown and Struever were fortunate in being able to treat each occupation level of this mammoth site as an entirely separate digging operation.

The archaeologists had two options. One was to dig small test trenches and obtain samples of pottery and other finds from each stratigraphic level. But this approach, though cheaper and commonly used, was inadequate for the problems to be investigated at the Koster site. The excavators were interested in studying the origins of agriculture in the lower Illinois Valley. Brown and Struever therefore decided to excavate each living surface on a sufficiently large scale to study the activities that had taken place there. This procedure would enable them to examine minute economic changes. Thus, the emphasis in the Koster excavations was on isolating the different settlement types that lay one on top of the other.

In developing the Koster research design, Brown and Struever needed to control a mass of complex variables that affected their data. They had to invent special procedures to ensure the statistical validity of their excavations. In order to acquire immediate feedback on the finds made during the excavations, they organized an elaborate data-processing system that sorted the animal bones, artifacts, vegetable remains, and other discoveries on location in the field. The tabulated information on each sorted find was then fed by remote access terminal to a computer many miles away. Within a few days, the excavators had instant access to the latest data from the dig. This system means that overall research design can be modified while an excavation is still in progress.

The Koster site is a fine example of elaborate research design that uses complex computer technology. The dig employed dozens of people each field season. Most excavations operate on a far smaller scale, but the ultimate principles are the same: sound research design, very careful recording of all data, and scientifically controlled excavation. The Koster excavation was designed, like all good digs, to solve specific research problems formulated in the context of a sound research design.

## TYPES OF EXCAVATION

How do you decide where to dig? What tools do you use, and why are your trenches in this shape? How deep do you excavate? People always seem to ask these same questions when they visit an excavation. Below we discuss different types of archaeological sites and the problems they create for excavators. Here now are some general principles.

You can decide where to dig on a site by simple, arbitrary choice of a spot that has yielded a large number of surface finds or one where traces of stone walls or other ancient structures can be seen above ground. When Richard Daugherty dug the Ozette site on the Washington coast, he began by digging through the place where the largest occupation sequence seemed to be. Why? He needed to obtain as complete a cultural sequence as he could. The logical way to do so was to dig through the deepest part of the site. There was, of course, no guarantee that his trench would penetrate to the earliest part of the whale hunters' site. But his choice was a logical way to start attacking the fundamental questions of when and for how long the whale hunters lived at Ozette. Similar decisions have been made at thousands of other sites all over the world.

In these days of high digging costs, archaeologists rely more heavily on statistical sampling than their predecessors did. Sampling is used in digging shell heaps or dense accumulations of occupation debris containing thousands of artifacts. Obviously only a small sample of a large garbage heap can be dug and analyzed. To ensure validity of the statistical samples, some form of sampling technique must be used to choose which part of a site is to be dug in an unbiased way.

**Sampling** has been defined as the "science of controlling and measuring the reliability of information through the theory of probability." Sampling techniques allow us to ensure a statistically reliable basis of archaeological data from which we can make generalizations about our research data. Most archaeologists make use of **probabilistic sampling**, for the discipline of statistics and statistical theory makes considerable use of probability theory, a means of relating small samples of data in mathematical ways to much larger populations. The classic example of this technique is the political opinion poll, testing national feelings from tiny samples, perhaps as few as 1,500 people. In archaeology probabilistic sampling improves the likelihood that the conclusions reached from a survey or excavation on the basis of the samples are relatively reliable.

The use of formal sampling techniques in archaeology is still in an initial stage. Simple **random sampling** is quite commonly used, as when an archaeologist wishes to obtain an unbiased sample of artifacts from an ancient shell mound. One can arrive at this result by laying out a rectangular grid of squares on a site and then selecting the squares to be dug

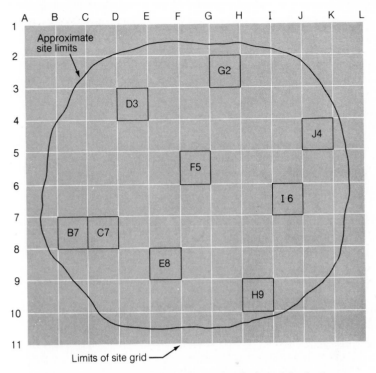

FIGURE 6.1  A hypothetical dig with trenches laid out by referring to a random sampling table. That is, the trench layout is completely by chance, with the cuttings to be dug selected from a table of randomly selected numbers.

by using a table of random numbers (Figure 6.1). The excavated samples are thus chosen at random, rather than on the basis of surface finds or other considerations. Then there is **stratified sampling**, where the investigator uses previous knowledge of an area, such as its topographic variation, to structure further research. This selection enables one to sample some sample units intensively, others less thoroughly. Archaeological sampling, based as it is on descriptive and inferential statistics, is a complex subject that is still in its infancy. I urge you to consult the references at the back of this book.

FIGURE 6.2　Vertical excavation in Coxcatlán Cave in Tehuacán Valley, Mexico. The large pits result from the excavation of alternate squares as separate units. Coxcatlán has yielded some of the earliest evidence of maize cultivation in the world.

## Vertical Excavation

The layout of small digs is determined not only by surface features, density of surface finds, or sampling techniques, but by available funds as well. Most excavations are run on shoestring budgets, and so small-scale operations have to be used to solve complex problems with minimal expenditure of time and money. Some of the world's most important sites, such as Coxcatlán Cave in the Tehuacán Valley, Mexico (Figure 6.2), have been excavated on a small scale by vertical excavation, digging limited areas for specific information on dating and stratigraphy. Vertical trenches can be used to obtain artifact samples, to establish sequences of ancient building construction or histories of complex earthworks, and to salvage sites threatened with destruction. The small trenches are often dug in areas where the deposits are likely to be of maximal thickness or where important structures may be found. Much vertical excavation is test trenching, designed to establish the cultural sequence at, and extent of, a site before area excavation begins.

### Area Excavation

Large-scale excavations are normally used to uncover wider areas of a site. These horizontal, or area, excavations are used to uncover house plans and settlement layouts. They are expensive (Figure 6.3). The only sites that are completely excavated are very small hunter-gatherer camps, isolated huts, or burial mounds. With larger settlements, all one can do is excavate several portions of the settled area, in order to sample areas representative of the entire settlement.

Area excavations expose large, open areas of ground to a depth of several feet. A complex network of walls or abandoned storage pits may lie within the area to be investigated. Each of these ancient features relates to other structures, a relationship that must be carefully recorded if the site is to be interpreted correctly. If the area excavated is large, we immediately have a big recording problem. The excavators use a grid of squares, each with its own letter and number, to aid in digging and recording the site (Figure 6.4a). For excavating the surviving remains of an Indian long house or a scatter of artifacts left by a prehistoric craftsman, accurate recording techniques are obviously essential (Figure 6.4b).

## DIGGING, TOOLS, AND PEOPLE

How do you do the digging? Much depends on the type of site you are excavating. A huge burial mound on the Ohio River may be more than twenty feet long. Much of the sterile deposit covering the burial levels is removed with picks and

FIGURE 6.3   Area excavation of an Iroquois long house near Onondaga, New York. The small stakes indicate positions of house wall posts; placement of hearth areas and support posts can be seen inside the walls.

shovels. But as soon as the archaeologists reach layers where finds are expected, they dig with meticulous care, removing each layer in turn, recording the exact position of their finds upon discovery. Smaller caves or cemeteries are excavated inch by inch. The earth surrounding the finds is passed through fine screens so that tiny beads, fish bones, and myriad small items can be found.

Excavation is in part a recording process, and accuracy is essential. The records will never be precise unless the dig is kept tidy at all times. The trench walls must always be straight. Why? So that you can record the layers you are digging and follow them across the site. Surplus soil is dumped well away from the trenches so that it does not cascade into the dig or have to be shifted when new areas are opened up. The excavation is a laboratory and should be treated as such.

All archaeological digs are headed by a director, who is

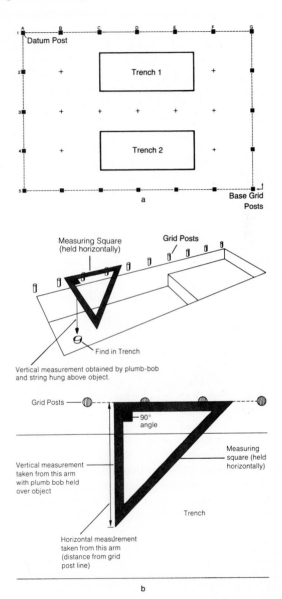

FIGURE 6.4 (a) Two trenches laid out with a grid. (b) Three-dimensional recording of the position of an object, using the grid squares.

responsible both for organizing the excavation and for over-
seeing the specialists and diggers under her or his supervision. Many larger digs will involve a team of specialist experts
who work alongside the excavators. At the Ozette site, Richard Daugherty had the cooperation of a geologist and a zo-
ologist who visited the site regularly. They studied the geological background of the settlement and the many animal
bones found as the dig proceeded. A really large excavation
in Mesopotamia or Mesoamerica can involve dozens of people—specialist archaeologists, a team of resident experts in
other fields, graduate student trainees, and volunteer or paid
workers who do much of the actual excavation. We describe
some of the ways in which you can obtain digging experience
in Chapter 10.

Archaeologists use many digging tools in their work. Picks,
shovels, and long-handled spades carry the brunt of the
heavy work. But the most common archaeological tool is the
diamond-shaped trowel, with its straight edges and sharp tip.
With it, soil can be eased from a delicate specimen or an
unusual discoloration in the soil scraped clean. Trowels are
used for tracing delicate layers in walls, clearing small pits,
and other fine jobs. They are rarely out of the digger's hand.

Household and paint brushes often come in handy, the
former for soft, dry sediments, and for cleaning trenches, and
the latter for freeing fragile objects from the soil. Even fine
artists' brushes have their uses, for cleaning beads, decaying
ironwork, or fine bones in human burials. Enterprising archaeologists visit their dentists regularly, if only to obtain regular supplies of worn-out dental instruments, which make
first-rate fine digging tools! And so do six-inch nails ground
to different shapes. A set of fine screens for sifting soil for
small finds, several notebooks and graph paper, tapes, plumb
bobs, surveyors' levels, and a compass are just a few of the
items that archaeologists need to record their excavations and
to process their finds.

## RECORDING

No dig is worth more than its records. The excavation notebooks provide a day-to-day record of each trench, of new

layers and significant finds. Before any trench is measured out, the entire site is laid out on a grid of squares. Important finds, or details of a house or a storage pit, are measured in on the site plan by simple, three-dimensional recording techniques (Figure 6.4b). It is information from your records, as well as the artifacts from the dig, that form the priceless archive of your excavation. If the records are incomplete, the dig is little better than a treasure hunt.

Let us now turn from general principles to some specific excavation problems that will give you an insight into the multitude of challenges awaiting field workers. As we indicated in Chapter 2, archaeological sites, in all shapes and sizes, are the basis for all field investigations. All contain traces of human activity, in the form of artifacts, structures, and food remains. Archaeologists most commonly classify sites by their functions; that is to say, by the activities that took place within them. It is no coincidence that these various site categories present different excavation problems.

## HABITATION SITES

### Open Campsites and Villages

Habitation sites are the most common archaeological sites, places where people have lived and carried out many activities. Hunter-gatherers have occupied temporary camps for short periods since the very earliest millennia of prehistory. Where preservation conditions are good, archaeologists can sometimes identify such settlements, represented by concentrations of stone artifacts and broken animal bones, as well as the stone foundations of long-abandoned brush shelters. Such concentrations have been found in the Great Basin of the American West, in the arctic north, and also in sub-Saharan Africa.

Many hunter-gatherer camps are hard to identify from the surviving archaeological record (Figure 6.5). The same is not true of later farming villages, which were usually occupied longer, enabling considerable quantities of occupation debris,

FIGURE 6.5  Excavation of an artifact and bone concentration at Olduvai Gorge, Tanzania. The interpretation of such locations as habitation sites has caused considerable controversy. Recent research
suggests that many such early "campsites" may, in fact, have been
places where early hominids cached and processed meat and bones
scavenged from nearby predator kills.

as well as substantial house foundations, to accumulate.
Some 8,000 years ago, the villagers of Áin Ghazal in Jordan
lived in a large settlement of small huts and stock compounds
covering several acres. The house foundations and numerous
animal bones, as well as other artifacts, enabled the excavators to trace the extent of the settlement.

Numerous prehistoric agricultural settlements in North America were occupied over long periods, and in them varied domestic and industrial activities took place, as well as food preparation and household life (Figure 6.3).

## Caves and Rockshelters

The mouth of a cave or a rocky overhang in a cliff were favorite homes for prehistoric people. Huge accumulations of occupation debris extending over thousands of years are to be found in the great rockshelters and caves of the Dordogne Valley in southwest France, where prehistoric hunter-gatherers flourished from forty thousand to ten thousand years ago and painted exquisite pictures of the animals they hunted. Danger and Hogup Caves in Utah contain thousands of years of hunter-gatherer occupation. The dry environment of the desert preserved wood objects and basketry, as well as minute details of economic life. And the dry caves of Tehuacán Valley in south-central Mexico provide a unique history of how maize cultivation developed in the New World (Chapter 8).

Cave and rockshelter excavations are some of the hardest digs to carry through successfully. The ground below the cliff overhangs usually consists of ash and other debris piled up through successive human occupations. Sterile soils may interrupt this sequence of habitation, representing periods when the site was abandoned. Excavating such complicated sequences is slow and meticulous work. The trenches are usually restricted by the size of the shelter. Each hearth and small occupation layer has to be isolated from the others during excavation.

Many cave and rockshelter excavations, deal purely with dating and stratigraphy, but others are more ambitious. When Hallam Movius dug the Abri Pataud rockshelter in France, he had to record at least six layers of human occupation dated to between forty thousand and nine thousand years ago, extending to more than twenty feet of stratified deposit. The site was excavated following a coordinated master plan that involved not only archaeologists but botanists, geologists, and other specialists as well. Movius was able to record minute changes in tool types and to record many de-

FIGURE 6.6   Tepe Yahya, Iran, a typical Near Eastern city mound, or
*tell*. The stepped trenches of the excavation can be seen in the slope
of the mound.

tails of the changing hunting and gathering practices of Abri
Pataud's inhabitants.

## Mounds

Occupation mounds (often called "tells" in the Near East)
are common in many parts of the world. Mound sites result
when the same site is occupied for centuries, even thousands
of years. Successive generations lived atop their predecessors'
settlements. The result is a gradual accumulation of occupation debris, which, when excavated, provides a complicated picture of occupation levels.

Even a small mound can cost a fortune to excavate, simply
because the lowest levels are so deeply buried below the surface. A huge mound like that of Ur-of-the-Chaldees in Mesopotamia, or Tepe Yahya in Iran, can be sampled only by
large trenches that cut into the sides of the mound in a series
of great steps, or by very large-scale excavation indeed, using
a combination of vertical and area trenches (Figure 6.6). There
is far more to excavating an occupation mound than merely

FIGURE 6.7   The Iron Age hill fort at Maiden Castle, Dorset, England; its extensive earthworks were excavated by Mortimer Wheeler.

stripping off successive occupation layers. So many natural and artificial processes, ranging from wind erosion to human activity, can change the stratigraphy of a site of this type that each site presents a challenging new excavation problem.

## Earthworks and Forts

Many peoples—Iron Age peasants in western Europe, Maori warriors in New Zealand, Hopewell Indians in Ohio— built extensive earth fortifications to protect their settlements or sacred places. The Ohio earthworks enclose large areas of ground, but no one knows exactly why such earthworks were undertaken. To excavate them would require both vertical excavation to record cross-sections across the earthworks, and area investigation to uncover the layout of the structures built inside the earthworks. Such excavations were indeed carried out on the great prehistoric fortress at Maiden Castle, England, many years ago. The massive earthworks of Maiden Castle were stormed by a Roman legion in A.D. 43. By careful excavation and use of historical data, the excavator Mortimer Wheeler was able to write a blow-by-blow description of the battle for the fortress (Figure 6.7).

FIGURE 6.8  An exemplary area excavation of a shallow shell midden at Galatea Bay, New Zealand.

## Shell Middens

Shell middens, which are vast accumulations of abandoned shells, fish bones, and other food remains, are common in many coastal areas of the world. Remarkable results can be attained by studying these dense heaps, especially in reconstructing prehistoric diets (Chapter 8). The excavation problem is twofold: first, to identify the stratified levels in the middens, and second, to obtain statistically reliable samples of food remains and artifacts from the deposits. Most shell midden digs are laid out by random cuttings, described very briefly earlier. We illustrate an example of an area excavation on a New Zealand shell midden (Figure 6.8), where much information on ancient diet was found by using a carefully laid-out grid of trenches. The excavation of a shell midden is mostly rather unspectacular, for the detailed statistical results come from laboratory analysis of artifacts rather than from actual digging. One hopes to look at ways in which the inhabitants utilized different communities of shellfish, such as oysters of different sizes, through time.

## CEREMONIAL AND OTHER SPECIALIST SITES

Some of the world's most famous archaeological sites are ceremonial centers like the pyramids of Giza in Egypt or the Maya ceremonial center at Copán, Honduras. Many ceremonial sites are enormous, and, like occupation mounds, present great difficulties for the excavator. Teotihuacán in the Valley of Mexico is, of course, far more than a ceremonial center (see Figure 9.1). It was a great city as well, which flourished from 200 B.C. to as late as A.D. 750. Discovering the true significance of the site has involved not only extensive area excavation designed to help reconstruct pyramids and major buildings, but sophisticated mapping and surface survey combined with small-scale excavation as well. René Millon and other archaeologists have mapped more than twelve and a half square miles of Teotihuacán in a survey program combined with some excavation. Their aim is to give a comprehensive picture of the huge city as it rapidly developed into a religious and ceremonial center of wide importance.

With trading sites, quarries and other specialized sites, as well as with ceremonial centers, indeed all sites, one major question is the artifact patternings coming from the excavations. Do these patterns reflect long-distance trading activity in, say, copper ornaments or seashells? Are marine sting-ray spines, which are present in ruins that appear to be temples built hundreds of miles inland, artifacts of great religious significance in Mexico? It is questions like these that can be answered only by careful studies of artifact patterning.

## BURIALS AND CEMETERIES

Human burials are the stereotypic finds of archaeology, reflecting humanity's abiding concern with the afterlife. The earliest human burials were left by Neanderthal peoples more than seventy thousand years ago. Most human societies have paid careful attention to funerals and burials ever since. Many burials were deposited with simple or elaborate grave furniture, designed to accompany its owner to the afterlife.

People have buried their dead in isolated, shallow graves within their settlement, in special cemeteries, in caves, cremated in jars, and in vast burial mounds. Some burials consist of skeleton alone, others lie with a few beads or a handful of clay pots (Figure 6.9). Royal personages have been buried in all their glory: Shang kings in China with their chariots; the rulers of early Ur-of-the-Chaldees, Mesopotamia, with their entire court; Maya nobles with their prize treasures

By studying a group of burials from one cemetery, it may be possible to distinguish different social classes by the grave furniture buried with the skeleton. The common people may take nothing with them, and merchants or priests may be buried with distinctive artifacts associated with their status in society. The Adena and Hopewell peoples of North America were much concerned with the afterlife during their heyday two thousand years ago. From the distribution of the burials and cemeteries in their burial mounds, and from the cult objects and ornaments associated with the skeletons, it may be possible to gain some insights into the social organization of Adena and Hopewell societies (Chapter 9). And, of course, burials are a fruitful source of information on personal ornamentation and appearance, too, for people were (and still are) often buried in the clothes and ornaments they wore in life. The physical characteristics of the skeletons themselves can provide valuable data on age, nutrition, sex, and ancient disease.

How does one excavate a burial? Whether one is digging a large cemetery or a lone burial, each skeleton and its associated grave, ornaments, and grave goods are considered a single excavation problem. Each burial is dug as a unit that has both internal associations with its accompanying goods and external associations with other burials in the same and other levels. The first step is to identify the grave, either by locating a gravestone or a pile of stones, or from the grave outlines, which may appear as a discoloration in the surrounding soil. Once the grave outlines have been found, individual bones are exposed. The main outline of the burial is traced first. Then you uncover the fingers, toes, and other small bones. You leave the bones in place and take care not

FIGURE 6.9   A classic Maya collective tomb at Guattan in the Motagua Valley, Guatemala.

to displace any ornaments or grave furniture associated with them. Once the skeleton is exposed and fully cleaned where it lies, the layout of the burial and grave furniture is recorded by drawings and photographs before the skeleton is lifted bone by bone or encased in a cocoon of plaster of paris and metal strips (Figure 6.9).

Burial excavation may seem very romantic. In reality it is not only technically demanding, but raises important ethical questions as well. For years archaeologists casually dug up Indian burials, many of them only a few generations old. Now Indians are objecting strenuously to excavation and destruction of ancient burial grounds—and with good reason. They argue: Why should their ancestors be dug up and displayed in museums? Many surviving communities retain strong emotional and religious ties with their ancestors, links that must be respected by archaeologist, developer, and historian alike.

# 7

# ORDERING THE PAST

Order is Heav'n's first law

ALEXANDER POPE, *An Essay on Man*

## BACK FROM THE FIELD

Archaeologists spend much more time in their laboratories than they do excavating and surveying. They must, for the finds from even a brief excavation can take months to sort, classify, and analyze. The field crew returns from the dig with truckloads of boxes and bags of unsorted stone tools, pot fragments, broken animal bones, and other finds. Precious cartons contain human skeletons and rows of radiocarbon and soil samples for specialists to examine. It can take some days simply to organize these piles of boxes in the laboratory before the real work begins. Then, once the tables are clear, the long work of describing and ordering all the finds from the dig starts.

The laboratory crew—normally graduate students and undergraduates working under supervision—begin by sorting all the finds into very broad categories. Soil and radiocarbon samples are sent off to experts. Animal bones, seeds, and other food remains are separated from manufactured artifacts and handed over to the members of the team who are skilled in identifying such finds. The manufactured artifacts are sorted into broad classes, pot fragments separated from stone implements, metal tools handled separately from shell beads, and so on. The labeling of every bag and box is carefully checked. Properly marked containers must specify the three-dimensional unit of space and time in which the materials were found (see Figure 6.4). Everything is now ready for basic classification and ordering of the manufactured artifacts. In this chapter we describe some of the ways in which archaeologists tackle these complex tasks.

## CLASSIFICATION, TAXONOMY, AND SYSTEMATICS

Our attitude toward life and our surroundings involves constantly classifying and sorting massive quantities of data. We classify types of eating utensils: knives, forks, and spoons; each type has a different use and is kept in a separate compartment in the kitchen drawer. We group roads according to their surface, finish, and size. A station wagon is classified separately from a truck. As we classify artifacts, lifestyles, and cultures, we make choices among them. Most Westerners eat rice with a fork. But the Chinese and other Asian people use chopsticks, and still others have decided that a spoon is more suitable for the purpose. A variety of choices are available. The final decision is often dictated by cultural usage rather than functional pragmatism.

Everyone "classifies" because doing so is a requirement for abstract thought and language. Archaeological classification is something quite different, for classification is used as a research tool. All classifications used by archaeologists follow directly from the problems that they are studying. Let us say that a prehistorian is studying changes in pottery designs over a five-hundred-year period in the Southwest. The classification he or she uses will follow not only from what other people have done, but also from the problems being studied. How, and even what, you classify stems directly from the research questions asked about the data.

*Taxonomy* is a system for classifying concepts and terms used in many sciences, including archaeology. The taxonomies of biology, botany, geology, and some other disciplines are highly sophisticated and often very rigid systems that were created in the nineteenth century and early in the twentieth. Many are now dated by today's sophisticated standards. In contrast, archaeology has built its own taxonomy of specialist terminologies and concepts quite haphazardly. British archaeologists refer to "cultures," North American scholars to "phases" (see page 141), and the French to "periods." Each term has basically the same meaning, but the subtle differences stem from cultural attitudes and from different field situations.

*Systematics* is essentially a way of creating units that can be used to categorize things as a basis for explaining archaeological or other phenomena. It is a means for creating units of classification within a scientific discipline. Biologists classify human beings within a hierarchy of classification constructed by Carl Linnaeus in the eighteenth century. Human beings are grouped in the *Kingdom* Animalia, in a classificatory hierarchy that passes through the *Class* Mammalia, ending up with the *Subspecies Homo sapiens sapiens*. This arbitrary biological classification consists of empirically defined units, each precisely described and related to the others. Archaeologists use systematics in much the same way, but their classifications are closely related to the problem being studied.

### Objectives of Classification

As we have said, classification in archaeology depends on the problem being studied. Four major objectives can be identified, however.

1. *Organizing data into manageable units.* This step is part of the preliminary data-processing operation, and it commonly involves separating finds on the basis of raw material (stone, bone, and so on) or artifacts from food remains. This preliminary ordering allows much more detailed classification later on.

2. *Describing types.* By identifying the individual features (attributes) of hundreds of artifacts, or clusters of artifacts, the archaeologist can group them, by common attributes, into relatively few types. These types are economical ways of describing large numbers of artifacts.

3. *Identifying relationships between types.* This procedure is done to provide a basis for formulating hypotheses about the meaning of the classification. The hierarchy of types orders the relationships between artifacts, which stem, in part, from

the use of a variety of raw materials, manufacturing techniques, and functions.

These three objectives are much used in culture-historical research (see page 19). Processual archaeologists may use classification for:

4. *Studying assemblage variability* in the archaeological record. These studies are often combined with middle-range research on dynamic, living cultural systems (see Chapter 10).

We must always be aware that archaeological classifications are artificial formulations that are based on criteria set up by archaeologists. *They do not necessarily coincide with those invented by the people who made the original artifacts.*

## Typology

Typology is the system of archaeological classification that is based on the comparison of types. It is a search for structure among either objects or the variables that define these objects, a search that has taken on added meaning and complexity as archaeologists have begun to use computer technology and sophisticated statistical methods.

Originally, archaeological typology involved arbitrarily dividing up objects and variables. The arbitrariness of this proceeding broke up the underlying patterning from which the structure was created, so that one lost the opportunity to examine underlying patterns of human design and behavior.

The value of typology is that it enables one to *compare* what has been found at two sites or in different levels of the same site. Typology has one main objective: classification to permit comparison, so that you can align your assemblage of artifacts or other finds in time and space.

Let us look over a group of archaeologists' shoulders as they sort through a large pile of potsherds, from one occupation level, on the laboratory table.

First the sherds are separated by decoration or lack of it, paste, temper, firing methods, and vessel shape. Once the undecorated or shapeless potsherds have been counted and weighed, they are put to one side, unless they have some special significance. Then the remaining sherds are examined individually and divided into types, according to the features they display. Soon, a number of piles are on the table: one consists of sherds painted with black designs; a second, of red-painted fragments; a third, a group of plain sherds that come from shallow platters. Once the preliminary sort is completed, the archaeologists look over each pile in turn. They have already identified three broad types in the pottery collection. But when they examine the first pile more closely, they find that the black-painted sherds can be divided into several smaller groupings: one with square, black panels; another with diamond designs; and a third with black-dotted decoration. The other two major piles also yield several subtypes. Eventually, the original three types become nine, as the archaeologists study the collection in minute detail, identifying dozens if not hundreds of attributes, conspicuous and inconspicuous, stylistic or dimensional, even some based on chemical analyses. These data are programmed into a computer in preparing for the quantitative analyses that will help sort out discrete types and variations between them. This is the process of typology, classifying artifacts so that you can compare one type with another. Obviously, the nine types from this one site can be compared with other arbitrary types found during laboratory sorting of collections from nearby sites.

For accurate and meaningful comparisons to be made, rigorous definitions of analytical types are needed, to define not only the "norm" of the artifact type but also its approximate range of variation, at either end of which one type becomes one of two others. Conventional analytical definitions are usually couched in terms of one or more attributes that indicate how the artifact was made, or the shape, or the decoration, or some other feature that the maker wanted the finished product to display. These definitions are set up following carefully defined technological differences, often bolstered by measurements or statistical clustering of attributes. Most often, the average artifact, rather than the variation between individual examples, is the ultimate objective of the definition. A classifier who finds a group, or even an individual artifact, which deviates at all conspicuously from the norm, often erects a new analytical type. Those who are splitters tend to proliferate types, and those who are lumpers do the opposite. The whole operation is more or less intuitive.

## Archaeological Classification

As we have emphasized, archaeological classification is the ordering of data according to shared characteristics. But how do archaeologists go about this organizing?

Typology is based on the archaeologist's "concept of types," a subject that is one of the great controversies in archaeology.

On a formal level, a *type* can be defined as a group or class of items that was internally cohesive and separated from other groups by one or more discontinuities. Beyond this most general definition, the experts are in profound disagreement. Most now argue that types are identified by combinations of attributes that distinguish and isolate one artifact type from another. In the final analysis, the idea is to organize data in such a way as to reveal continuities and breaks between groups of artifacts that display internal cohesion and are isolated from other such groups.

*Attributes* are the characteristics used to distinguish one artifact from another. As archaeologists work out their typologies, they find themselves examining hundreds of individual fragments, each of which bears several distinctive attributes (Figure 7.1). Back in our hypothetical laboratory, fifty sherds bear black-painted designs, eight have red panels on the neck, ten are flattened bowls, and so on. A potsherd may bear an everted lip, incised decoration applied in a cross-hatcned motif, and a red-painted surface. It may have a grit temper, bright red paste, and a slipped interior surface. Each of the many individual features is an attribute, most of them obvious enough. Only a critically selected few of these attributes, however, will be used in classifying the artifacts. (If all were used, then no classification would be possible: each artifact would be an individual object identified by several trivial manufacturing or design idiosyncrasies.) Remember about attributes that any artifact has an infinite range of them, and the archaeologist works with those considered most appropriate for the classificatory task at hand.

A number of broad groups of attributes are in common use:

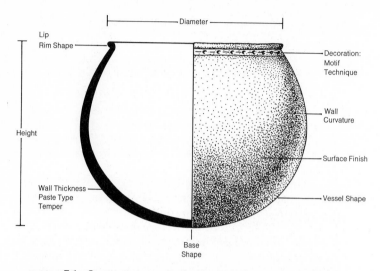

**FIGURE** 7.1   Some common attributes of a clay vessel. Specific attributes that could be listed for this pot are concave shoulder, dot and drag decoration, mica temper, round base, and thickness of wall at base.

*Form attributes* are such features as the shape of the artifact, its measurable dimensions, and its components. Normally, they are fairly obvious.

*Stylistic attributes* include decorations, color, surface finish, and so on.

*Technological attributes* are those covering the material used to make an artifact and the way it was made.

The selection of attributes usually proceeds through a close examination of a collection of artifacts. A group of potsherds can be divided into decorative styles based on shapes, surfaces, and colors. The selected attributes are then hand recorded, and a series of artifact types is erected from them.

## Archaeological Types

All of us have feelings and reactions about any artifact, whether it is a magnificent wood helmet from the Pacific

FIGURE 7.2 Tlingit carved wood helmet from the Northwest Coast, a "natural" type, classified as such when found in an archaeological context. This artifact would obviously be classified as a helmet from the perspective of our cultural experience. (Height, 9 inches; width, 10 inches.)

Northwest coast (Figure 7.2), or a simple acorn pounder from the southern California interior. Our immediate instinct is to look at and classify these and other prehistoric artifacts from our own cultural standpoint. That is, of course, what prehistoric peoples did as well. The owners of the tools that archaeologists study classified them into groups for themselves, each one having a definite role in their society. We assign different roles in eating to a knife, fork, and spoon. Knives cut meat, steak knives are used in eating steaks. The prehistoric arrowhead is employed in the chase; one type of missile head is used to hunt deer, another to shoot birds, and so on.

The use of an artifact may be determined not only by convenience and practical considerations, but by custom or regulation. The light-barbed spearheads used by some Australian hunting bands to catch fish are too fragile for dispatching kangaroo; with the special barbs the impaled fish can be lifted out of the water. Pots are made by women in most African or American Indian societies, which have division of labor by sex; each has formed complicated customs, regulations, or taboos, which, functional considerations apart, categorize clay pots into different types with varying uses and rules in the culture (Figure 7.3).

Furthermore, each society has its own conception of what an artifact should look like. Until recently, Americans have generally preferred larger cars, Europeans small ones. These preferences reflected not only pragmatic considerations of road width and longer distances in the New World, but also differing attitudes toward traveling. Many Americans still think that their car is a reflection of prestige and social standing. To these people, style changes, aluminum wheel designs, turbos, and other niceties are important. But we all think that a car should have a color coordinated interior to look "right." The steering wheel is on the left, and it is equipped with turn signals and seatbelts by law. In other words, we know what we want and expect an automobile to look like, even though minor design details change—as do the length of women's skirts and the width of men's ties.

The problem that confronts the archaeologist is to devise archaeological types that are appropriate to the research problems they are tackling, an extremely difficult task. In archaeology, a type is a grouping of artifacts created for comparison with other groups. This grouping may or may not coincide with the actual tool types designated by the original manufacturers. Everyone agrees that a type is based on clusters of attributes, or on clusters of objects.

Though patterns of attributes may be fairly easy to identify, how do archaeologists know what is a type and what is not? Should they try to reproduce the categories of pot that the makers themselves conceived? Or should they just go ahead and create quite arbitrary "archaeological" types designed purely for analytical purposes? This is the nub of the controversy about types in archaeology.

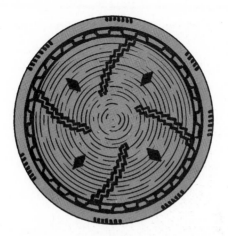

FIGURE 7.3  A Chumash parching tray.

A good example of the difficulties in archaeological classification. This finely made basket was produced by the Chumash Indians of southern California. It was made by weaving plant fibers. The design was formed in the maker's mind by several factors, most important of which is the tremendous reservoir of learned cultural experience that the Chumash have acquired, generation by generation, through the several thousand years they lived in southern California. The designs of their baskets are almost unconscious, and relate to the feeling that such and such a form and color are "correct" and traditionally acceptable. But there are more pragmatic and complex reasons, too, including the flat, circular shape that enables the user to roast seeds by tossing them with red embers.

Each attribute of the basket has a good reason for its presence—whether traditional, innovative, functional, or imposed by the technology used to make it. The band of decoration around the rim is a feature of the Chumash decorative tradition and occurs on most of their baskets. It has a rich red-brown color from the species of reed used to make it. The steplike decoration was dictated by the sewing and weaving techniques, but the diamond pattern is unique and the innovative stamp of one weaver, which might or might not be adopted by other craftspeople in later generations. The problem for the archaeologist is to measure the variations in human artifacts, and to establish the causes behind, and directions of change, and to find what these variations can be used to measure. This fine parching tray is a warning that variations in human artifacts are both complex and subtle.

Archaeologists tend to use four "types of types":

*Descriptive types* are the most elementary, descriptions based solely on the form of the artifact—physical or external properties. The descriptive type is used when the use or cultural significance of an object or practice is unknown. The excavations at *Snaketown* in Arizona revealed a "large, basin-like depression." This description "type" was subsequently proven to be a ball court, and so the noncommittal descriptive classification was abandoned in favor of a functional one that defined the structure's role in *Hohokam* culture. Descriptive types are commonly used in the earlier periods of archaeology, when functional interpretation is much harder to arrive at (Figure 7.4).

*Chronological types* are defined by form, but are time markers. They are types with chronological significance. Like descriptive types, they are part of a culture's inventory as reflected in the archaeological record, but are widely used to distinguish chronological and spatial differences. Pottery is probably the most common form of chronological type, for the clay, shape, decoration, and so on change, and are assumed to have noncultural significance and to be significant and historical indices. Thus pottery, stone artifacts, and other chronological types have become vital elements in building the cultural sequences constructed by culture historians.

Chronological types figure prominently in southwestern archaeology, and were used by Alfred Kidder in his classic excavations at *Pecos*.

*Functional types* are based on cultural use or role rather than on outward form or chronological position. The same artifacts can be treated as of the functional type or the descriptive one. You can classify an assemblage in broad categories: "wood," "bone," "stone," and so on. But equally well, you may adopt a functional classification: "weapons," "clothing," "food preparation," and so on.

Ideally, functional types should reflect the precise roles and functional classifications made by the members of the society from which they came. Needless to say, such an objective is

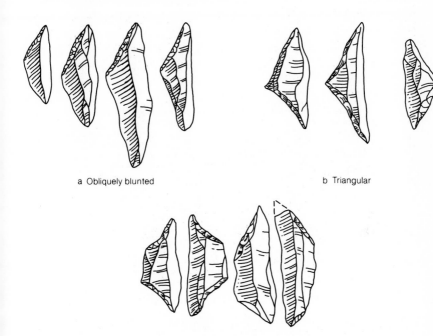

a  Obliquely blunted                    b  Triangular

c  Elongated trapeze

FIGURE 7.4  Nine-thousand-year-old Mesolithic artifacts from *Star Carr*, England (actual size). You can classify these by—Descriptive type: geometric stone tools; Chronological type: Mesolithic microliths, Star Carr forms; Functional type: microlithic arrowhead barbs.

very difficult to achieve, because of incomplete preservation and lack of written records. We have no means of visualizing the complex roles that some artifacts achieved in prehistoric society, or of establishing the restrictions placed on their use by the society (Figure 7.5).

*Stylistic types* are best exemplified by items like dress, because style is often used to convey information by displaying it in public. The Aztecs of central Mexico lived in a ranked society where everyone's dress was carefully regulated by sumptuary laws (Figure 7.6). Thus, a glance at the noble in the marketplace could reveal not only his rank but the num-

PASTE

*Tempering* Grit, diameters ranging from −0.5 to 2.0 mm. The appearance and composition (quartz, mica, and a little feldspar) suggest that the tempering material is a decomposed granite.

*Texture* Medium to coarse.

*Hardness* 3.0–4.0.

*Color* Tan to dark gray; exterior surfaces often heavily carboned.

FORM

*Overall shape* Jars with collared rims, constricted necks, rounded shoulders, and rounded bottoms.

*Lip* Rounded, occasionally thickened by the addition of a small bracing fillet on the exterior surface.

*Rim* All the rims are collared. The collars range from 24 to 55 mm. in height. Interior and exterior profiles are more or less parallel to each other, forming a straight or concave plane which extends downward and outward from the lip. The lower edge of the collar is marked by a fairly abrupt shoulder which forms the junction between the collar and the low curved neck. The bottom of the collar is sometimes scalloped. Below the neck, the vessel wall turns outward toward the shoulder. These rims might be contrasted with the rims of the Foreman types by describing them as Z-rims rather than S-rims, since the surface is flat or concave rather than convex.

*Neck* A relatively low, constricted zone below the shoulder of the rim.

*Shoulder* Rounded.

*Base* Rounded.

HANDLES One sherd has a short tablike lug extending down from the lower edge of the collar in the same plane as the face of the collar itself. Two others have fractured areas which seem to indicate the presence of loop handles running from the base of the rim collar to the shoulder of the vessel.

SURFACE FINISH Bodies simple stamped, some with extensive plain areas. The stamping on one of the restored vessels is vertical. Necks are plain or brushed vertically; interior surfaces are plain.

DECORATION The decoration is confined to the rim and lip. It is preponderantly cord impressed. Patterns consist of a series of horizontal lines, or a series of interlocking triangles filled alternately with horizontal and diagonal cord impressions. The cord-impressed zone is sometimes bordered by a series of punctations. Two pieces were decorated with diagonal broad-trailed lines, and one was plain except for a series of punctations at the base of the rim.

REMARKS A number of the pieces assigned to Colombe Collared Rim at the Phillips Ranch site show a considerable similarity to some Lower Loup sherds from Nebraska. The most striking difference is in the incised decoration on the Nebraska pieces and the predominantly cord-impressed decoration on the Phillips Ranch rims.

FROM: D. J. Lehmer, *Archaeological Investigations in the Oahe Dam Area, South Dakota, 1950–51*, Bureau of American Ethnology, Bulletin 158, 1954.

FIGURE 7.5 (At left.) An archaeologists's type description of a pottery type from South Dakota, "Colombe Collared Rim." This description appears exactly as it was published in 1954 by D. J. Lehmer. This example gives you an idea of the detail required for type description. Do not be dismayed if you do not understand some of the technical terms used; they are irrelevant to the main discussion of types in this text.

ber of prisoners he had taken in battle and many other subtle differences. Even the gods had their own regalia and costumes that reflected their roles in the pantheon. Stylistic types can be expected, theoretically at any rate, to have a structure entirely different from that of functional ones. As such, they

FIGURE 7.6 Aztec warriors wearing elaborate uniforms signifying different ranks, awarded according to the number of captives taken in battle. From the Codex Mendoza.

are not used often in archaeological classification, except when historical records are available.

*Statistical techniques and clustering of artifacts.* Researchers in the past thirty years have produced such massive quantities of new archaeological data that it is a full-time job to keep track of the myriad records and artifacts from old and new excavations and surveys. Fortunately, the digital computer and a battery of statistical techniques have come to our aid. Computers can be used to store information and to identify patterns of regularity on the artifacts. A computer data bank can be manipulated in such a way as to tell you the percentage, in a collection of projectile points in a Paleo-Indian collection stored in the computer, which have notched bases and chisel-like tips, or the percentage of painted bowls from a Hohokam assemblage that have turned-in rims.

Modern archaeology relies heavily on statistical methods as well as sampling techniques. Statistical procedures have two objectives in archaeology. The first of these, *descriptive statistics*, is a battery of standard procedures with which large bodies of data are reduced to manageable proportions. These include frequency distributions of artifact attributes and types, various forms of graphs, and measures (central tendency and dispersion; that is, means, modes, and medians). These enable one to establish clustering or dispersion of variables and measurement of degrees of variability.

The second objective, *inferential statistics*, provides systematic procedures for generating sensible conclusions about the whole when only a part is known. Archaeologists most often work with only samples of data, and therefore face a fundamental problem: How far can one generalize from sample findings? Common-sense inferences have been used for generations, but the great bodies of data now available make such approaches much less effective than before. A body of statistical tools has been developed that forms a process of reasoning from a sample statistic to a population as a whole. At issue here is the need to determine the chances of error when making inferences about a population as a whole. In other words, what are the probabilities that statistical decisions based on small samples of data are reliable?

Statistical methods enable archaeologists to organize their

data in an intelligible way, and also to attempt predictions as
to the probability that their inferences from small samples are
valid for larger populations.

## What do Assemblages and Patternings Mean?

For generations archaeologists studying culture history
classified artifacts into *assemblages,* associations of tools that
were thought to be contemporary. This approach assumed
that human culture had progressed through the millennia.
Thus artifact assemblages were merely traces of contemporary
cultural "species" that extended far back into prehistory. This
"organic" view of culture history saw assemblages of artifacts
as distinct categories, like organic species, which did not
modify their form from one context to the next. It was assumed in the organic approach that a specific cultural tradition leads to only one characteristic type of industry in the
archaeological record, an industry circumscribed in time and
space.

The organic view of the past is a highly organized scheme,
rather like the Medieval "Chain of Being" in early biology,
where every living thing had its place in the general scheme
of things.

American archaeologists have generally preferred a more
"cultural" perspective, in which artifact assemblages and
other traits from living societies have been studied over vast
areas of North America. They admit to a strong correlation
between the distribution of distinctive cultural forms and different environments. But observations based on living societies show that it is almost impossible to distinguish, from
artifact assemblages alone, between ethnic and social groups.
If this is cultural reality, what, then, do the empirical data
derived from prehistoric artifacts mean? Were conditions different in the past from today?

Some archaeologists, among them Lewis Binford, have at-
tacked this problem by studying living hunter-gatherer societies. Binford spent time among the Nunamiut caribou hunters of northern Alaska. There, he learned that the only way
to understand a living society's subsistence and material culture was to conceive of all their sites as part of a larger system. The Nunamiut had residential sites, and many other

kinds of sites used for specialized purposes. Thus, he argued, archaeologists have to identify the specific function of each site they examine, then fit the sites into a much larger, overall pattern of land use. Archaeology's basic unit is the site; the artifacts in it are part of an assemblage pattern that reveals the different behaviors that took place there. If archaeologists want to understand the dynamics of cultural systems like that of the Nunamiut in the past, they will have to study and interpret prehistoric living conditions, using such classificatory devices as typology, tool frequencies, and the relationships between tool debris and finished artifacts, as just some of their methods of doing so. Thus, the role of classification in archaeology is shifting away from "organic" viewpoints that see artifacts and cultures as finite in time and space, to new means of problem-oriented classification that concentrate not only on individual tools, but on entire assemblages and their patternings. But the data for interpreting these patterns must finally come from sources other than stone tools or potsherds. In other words, classification alone is meaningless, unless the classifications are interpreted in terms of other data. And here is where the study of contemporary societies, "middle-range research," is coming into its own (Chapter 10). Artifact classifications are still carried out, for the most part, with approaches meant for reconstructing culture history, formulations of time and space that owed much to functional classifications of artifacts based on common sense. At the same time, however, new explanatory frameworks based on theories of cultural evolution are providing new explanations of the past. They are designed to account for the structure and change that everyone can see in the archaeological record of the ages, phenomena that are far more dynamic and ever-changing than the more rigid classifications of earlier scholars imply. Robert Dunnell and other theorists have pointed out that these new explanatory frameworks render it unimportant when a new element in human culture such as, say, the plow, was invented or first appeared. What matters is how and why it becomes accepted and visible in the archaeological record. The challenge for the archaeologist is to devise new methods for classifying artifacts that enable us to identify processes of cultural evolution in the archaeological record. Research into this most fundamental of problems is still in its infancy.

## UNITS OF ORDERING

You recall from Chapter 4 that an assemblage is the diverse group of artifacts found together that reflects the shared activities of a community. This assemblage was found in a single site. You recall too that the site is the fundamental unit for all stratigraphic studies in archaeology. If time has passed, one can assume that at least some culture has taken place at a site.

Many archaeological sites, like the Star Carr location in England, consist of a single assemblage of artifacts and a single component—another arbitrary archaeological unit (Figure 7.7). A **component** is a large set of specific cultural features, including such things as a particular pottery design, which serve to distinguish the culture of the inhabitants of a particular occupation level. Sites that were occupied many times, like Hogup Cave in Utah, contain many components, each of them distinguished by a set of characteristic cultural features that separate them in time and space from other levels at the same site. The social equivalent of the archaeologist's component is the **community**.

Once our research team's analysis is completed, they may find they have only one component to deal with. If the site was occupied several times, they might have two or three. How do they compare these components with those from other, nearby sites? And how do they develop a sequence of occupation levels and cultures for their local area?

When all the artifact collections from the local area have been analyzed and classified to everyone's satisfaction, they are ordered in space and time with the aid of stratigraphic observations, seriation, cross-dating, and radiocarbon or tree-ring dates. We described both seriation and cross-dating in Chapter 3, techniques that place artifacts in chronological order, with the help of battleship curves and dated components. Figure 7.7 shows how our team joined ten sites into a local sequence, a chronological ordering built up from several multicomponent sites and some single-component settlements within the area. They were also able to obtain some radiocarbon dates to give an accurate chronology for the sequence.

When the team studied the distribution of their sites, they

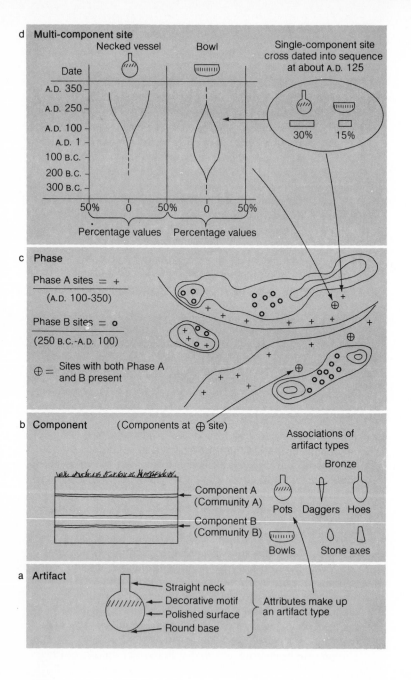

**d  Multi-component site**

Necked vessel

Bowl

Single-component site
cross dated into sequence
at about A.D. 125

Date

A.D. 350 –
A.D. 250 –
A.D. 100 –
A.D. 1 –
100 B.C. –
200 B.C. –
300 B.C. –

50%    0    50%    0    50%

30%    15%

Percentage values    Percentage values

**c  Phase**

Phase A sites = +
(A.D. 100-350)

Phase B sites = o
(250 B.C.-A.D. 100)

⊕ = Sites with both Phase A
and B present

**b  Component**    (Components at ⊕ site)

Associations of
artifact types

Bronze

Component A
(Community A)

Component B
(Community B)

Pots    Daggers    Hoes

Bowls    Stone axes

**a  Artifact**

← Straight neck
← Decorative motif
← Polished surface
← Round base

Attributes make up
an artifact type

140

FIGURE 7.7 (At left.) Archaeological units in use. (a) Patterns of attributes form an artifact type. (b) Cross-section through a hypothetical archaeological site with two stratified components. The two components are radiocarbon dated to between 250 B.C. and A.D. 100 and between A.D. 100 and 350 respectively. Our artifact type is a diagnostic vessel in Component A, the later one. The total artifact content from the site is the assemblage. (c) Now the archaeologists have studied dozens of sites in their archaeological region, which consists of an estuary with an offshore island. Higher ground with pine forest overlooks the estuary. When they plotted site distributions, they found that the earlier, Phase B sites were distributed on the higher ground, and the later components were established near the shore where shellfish were abundant. Only three sites contain both components, stratified one above the other. The two distributions are distinctive, both phases defined in space and time, forming a local sequence. (d) At the four two-component sites, the archaeologists seriated the pottery types and other artifacts and obtained distinctive battleship curves. Then they were able to fit other sites into the same sequence by cross-dating.

---

discovered that two different dated components were repeated at settlements over a considerable area. These were so well dated and precisely distributed in time that two phases in the sequence could be identified.

A **phase** is a cultural unit like a component and is made up of similar components on different sites. Instead of occurring at only one site, it is found at many settlements, though always within a well-defined chronological bracket. The characteristic artifacts of the phase may be found over hundreds of miles within the area covered by a local sequence. Many archaeologists use the term "culture" in the same sense as phase. Both are arbitrary terms designed to assist in ordering artifacts in time and space. Phases or cultures usually are named after a key site where characteristic artifacts are found. The *Acheulian* culture is named after the French town of St. Acheul, where the stone axes so characteristic of this culture are found (see Figure 5.1, p. 82).

### Larger Archaeological Units

After many seasons' work, our research team may have studied several local sequences and may be able to describe their finds in a wide context: the dozens of local sequences within the southwestern United States. Some characteristic art styles or artifacts, such as the *Chavín* art that flourished in Peru between 900 B.C. and 200 B.C., spread over enormous distances (Figure 7.8). Archaeologists have a number of larger-scale archaeological units that cover such situations. Perhaps the most renowned of these are the technological stages of prehistory identified by the Danish archaeologist Christian Jurgensen Thomsen in 1806. His Stone Age, Bronze Age, and Iron Age are technological labels still in wide use. For information on these and other larger-scale archaeological units, consult the "Further Reading" section at the back of this book.

## Explanatory Ordering

Our ordering of archaeological data is a descriptive process. It highlights the patterning and regularities in archaeological data. The concepts and units set forth above are devices used to organize data as a preliminary to studying culture change. These classificatory units put artifacts and other culture traits into a context of time and space developed by using distribution maps, stratigraphy, seriation and cross-dating, and chronometric dating methods.

So far we have talked of components, phases, and other units as phenomena in isolation. We have assumed that the artifacts they contain reflect gradual, evolutionary change in human society. But the archaeological record does not invariably reflect an orderly and smooth chronicle of culture change. A radical, new artifact inventory may suddenly appear in components at several sites, while earlier toolkits suddenly vanish. The economy of sites in a local sequence may change completely within a century as the plow revolutionizes agricultural methods. Such changes are readily observed in thousands of local sequences all over the world. But how did these changes come about? What processes of cultural change were at work to cause major and minor alterations in the archaeological record? It is here that the archaeologist turns from description of the past to explanation—to the study of cultural process.

FIGURE 7.8 A Chavín carving on a pillar in the temple interior at Chavín de Huantar, Peru. This reconstruction makes the temple walls rather more regular, and the background more open than they actually were.

## CULTURAL PROCESS

Cultural process consists of changes in human history. We recognize a number of primary cultural processes that have

143

operated specifically in human prehistory, any one of which can be invoked to account for changes in the archaeological record. These are inevitable variation, cultural selection, invention, diffusion, and migration.

### Inevitable Variation and Cultural Selection

**Inevitable variation** is rather similar to the well-known phenomenon of genetic drift in biology. As people learn the behavior patterns of their society, inevitably some minor differences in learned behavior will appear from generation to generation, which, minor in themselves, accumulate over a long time, especially in isolated populations. The snowball effect of inevitable variation and slow-moving cultural evolution can be detected in dozens of prehistoric societies. The great variation in Acheulian hand ax technology throughout Europe and Africa between a million and 150,000 years ago can be explained in part by the effects of inevitable variation.

Inevitable variation often results from isolation, a very low density of humans per square mile. It should not be confused with broad trends in human prehistory that grew over long periods. The more and more complex burial rituals in the Adena and Hopewell cultures of the American Midwest between 500 B.C. and A.D. 300 probably resulted from trends toward greater complexity in religious beliefs and rituals, as well as from political and economic organization, over a long time, not from isolation.

Inevitable variation is also quite different from what happens when a society recognizes that certain culture changes or inventions may be advantageous. Presumably, many hunter-gatherer societies deliberately took up cultivating the soil once they saw the advantages it gave neighboring peoples, who had already adopted the new economies (see discussion on diffusion on page 145).

### Invention

**Invention** is the creation or evolution of a new idea. Many inventions, such as new social institutions or religious beliefs, leave no trace in the archaeological record. But some innovations are reflected in new types of surviving artifacts, such as the plow, or an iron ax. If an invention such as plowing is sufficiently useful to be attractive to more than a few people, the new idea or a product of the idea will spread widely, and often rapidly.

Archaeologists have studied ways in which inventions spread by tracing the distribution of such distinctive artifacts as plowshares from their place of origin. The earliest occurrence of ironmaking is in northern Turkey about 1500 b.c. Iron tools first appear in the archaeological record of Europe and Egypt very much later. Because the earliest dated iron artifacts occur in Turkey, we can say that ironmaking was invented there.

In the early days of archaeology, people assumed that metallurgy and other major inventions were invented in only one place—in many cases, the Near East. These innovations then spread all over the world as other societies realized how important the new ideas were. But as the importance of environment and adaptation in the development of human culture have become better understood, this simple view of invention has been rejected. Agriculture is now known to have developed quite independently in the Near East, Southeast Asia, Mesoamerica, and Peru. Complex adaptive processes occurred in all these areas. Scholars now try to identify the many interacting factors that caused people to modify their life-styles to adopt food production. The genius of humanity was that it recognized opportunities when they came along and adapted to new circumstances. The issue is not who first cultivated the corncob but rather to study the dozens of major and minor alterations in human culture that were the result of adaptive changes over time.

### Diffusion

The spread of ideas, over short or long distances is **diffusion**. Ideas can be transmitted in many ways other than by the movements of entire societies or communities. Regular trade between neighboring villages or more distant peoples results in the exchange not only of goods, but of ideas as well, especially when much of this trade is conducted reciprocally. Reciprocity implies a two-sided relationship, in which both parties exchange goods, services, and of course, ideas.

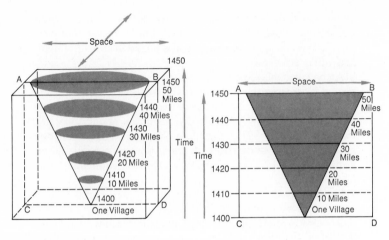

FIGURE 7.9    The spread of a culture trait in time and space: the cone effect.

Ideas such as a new religious belief are transmitted from individual to individual and ultimately from group to group. But neither the exchange of ideas nor that of technological innovations necessarily involve actual movements of people. Even the spread of material objects and abstract ideas can have a quite different effect in a new area. The classic example is that of the Hopi Indians of the Southwest. They received American trade goods but still retained their own culture, trading objects but rejecting the ideas of an alien culture.

Let us say that a new type of painted pot is invented in one village in A.D. 1400. The advantages of this new vessel are such that villagers ten miles away learn about it at a beer party five years later. Within ten years, their potters are making similar receptacles. In a short time the pot form is found commonly in villages ten miles farther away. Half a century later, communities in a fifty-mile radius are making the now well-established vessel design. If we put this stirring tale on paper, we end up with the cone effect shown in Figure 7.9. The cone effect is the type of distribution we study when identifying diffusion in the archaeological record.

Archaeologically, diffusion is difficult to identify unless one can use very distinctive artifacts obviously of common origin to demonstrate that the artifacts were invented in only one place, and trace the distribution of the artifact in space and time from its origin point to neighboring areas. To do so means establishing that the tool was first made in one place and that other sites nearby are later (Figure 7.9). Instances of diffusion in prehistory are common. A classic example is the *Chavín* art style of Peru, which diffused widely over the lowlands from a homeland in the highlands, where it appeared in about 900 B.C.

## Migration

**Migration** involves movements of entire societies that deliberately decide to expand their sphere of influence. English settlers moved to North America, taking their own culture with them. Spanish conquistadors occupied Mexico. Migration involves not only the movement of ideas but a mass shift of people that results in social and cultural changes on a large scale. A classic prehistoric migration was that of the Polynesians, who deliberately voyaged from island to island. In each case, new land masses were found by purposeful exploration, then colonized by small numbers of people who moved to an uninhabited island.

These types of mass migration are rare in prehistoric times. They would be reflected in the archaeological record by totally new components and phases or by skeletons of a totally new physical type. To be proved, the migration would have to show up as similar breaks in the cultural sequence at many sites in neighboring local sequences.

A second type of migration is on a smaller scale, when a group of foreigners move into another region and settle there as an organized group. A group of Oaxacans did just that at *Teotihuacán* in the Valley of Mexico. When René Millon mapped the whole of this remarkable city, he found a concentration of distinctive Oaxacan artifacts in one residential area. This Oaxacan colony flourished for centuries in an alien city. In this and many other cases, the immigrants adopt some features of the host culture but retain their own cultural identity.

There are other types of migration, too. Slaves and artisans are often unorganized migrants, sometimes taking new technological devices with them. Great warrior migrations, like those of Zulu regiments in South Africa in the early nineteenth century, can cause widespread disruption and population shifts. Such migrations leave few traces in archaeological sites. Within a few generations, the warriors settle down and adopt the sedentary life of the conquered. Only a few new weapon forms reveal the presence of strangers.

## Cultural Ecology and Cultural Process

As is obvious, great amounts of data are needed to identify invention, diffusion, or migration in the archaeological record. The *identification* of these classic cultural processes is largely a mechanical, descriptive activity because the artifacts used, be they stone axes, pots, or swords, are considered in isolation, and not as an element of the cultural system of which they are part. The *explanation* of culture change requires more sophisticated research models, based on the notion that human cultural systems are made up not only of many complex interacting elements—religious beliefs, technology, subsistence, and so on—but that these cultural systems also interact with the natural environment and other complex systems.

**Cultural ecology** is a means of studying human culture that gives a picture of the way in which human populations adapt to, and transform, their environments. Human cultural systems have to adapt to other cultures and also to the natural environment. So many factors influence cultural systems, indeed, that the processes by which cultural similarities and differences are generated are not easy to understand. Cultural ecologists see human cultures as subsystems interacting with other major subsystems, among them the biotic community and the physical environment. Thus, the key to understanding cultural process lies in the interactions between these various subsystems. Human culture is, ecologically speaking, the way in which humans compete successfully with other animals, plants, and other humans. But even though the number of probable adaptations to a specific environment is limited, human responses to different environments will be different and distinctive. Thus, communities with highly distinctive cultures may occupy the same or similar environments.

Many archaeologists have started to use cultural ecology to hypothesize about such major developments in world prehistory as the origins of agriculture and civilization. Kent Flannery has argued that a whole set of complex variables—economic, technological, religious, social, and environmental—affected the behavior of the first Sumerian city dwellers in Mesopotamia. Trade did not cause urban life, nor did religious beliefs alone, he argues. One has to look for the ways in which societies of the time regulated cultural change, the numerous interlocking checks and balances that encouraged and discouraged culture change. Many of these factors are intangible ideas or values that are hard to find in an archaeological site.

In the study of cultural process, the ultimate objective is to establish the rules by which a society ordered itself and permitted cultural change. We have only to look at our own society to see how many roadblocks can lie in the way of even simple changes in our way of living. In the pages that follow, we look at some of the ways in which archaeologists have tried to examine intangible parts of prehistoric cultural systems.

# 8

# SUBSISTENCE

There was a noise, and behold a shaking, and the bones came together, bone to his bone.

And when I beheld, lo, the sinews and the flesh came up upon them, and the skin covered them above, but there was no breath in them.

EZEKIEL 37:7–8

We now consider one of the most fascinating questions in archaeology: How did prehistoric peoples make their living? Once archaeologists realized that human prehistory was the story of humanity's diverse and constantly changing adaptations to world environments, they could not afford to ignore prehistoric subsistence activities, the ways in which people had fed themselves and achieved a satisfactory diet.

When studying prehistoric subsistence, the archaeologist seeks to answer many fundamental questions, among them these: What was the role of domestic animals in a mixed farming economy? How important was fishing to a shellfish-oriented population living by the ocean? Was a site occupied seasonally while the inhabitants concentrated on, say, bird snaring, to the exclusion of all other subsistence activities? What agricultural systems were used? How was the land cultivated? In this chapter we review some of the ways in which we seek the answers to these and related subsistence questions.

## EVIDENCE FOR SUBSISTENCE

The archaeological evidence for prehistoric subsistence consists of artifacts and food remains. How much survives de-

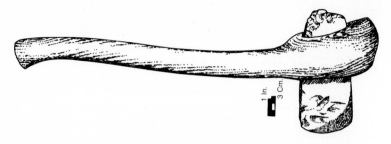

FIGURE 8.1 A reconstructed stone ax used by early Danish farmers for forest clearance. Such artifacts tell us little about prehistoric economic practices.

pends, of course, on preservation conditions on the site. All too often the evidence for ancient diet is incomplete. Stone axes or iron hoe blades may give an indication of hunting or agriculture, but they hardly yield the kind of detail archaeologists need. Many vital artifacts used in the chase or for agriculture were made from such perishable materials as bone, wood, and fiber (Figure 8.1).

Food remains themselves survive very unevenly. The bones and teeth of larger mammals are the most common economic data, but careful excavation will often reveal remains of such small animals as birds, fish, and frogs, as well as invertebrates like beetles. Vegetal remains are very perishable, and are usually underrepresented.

## PREHISTORIC DIET

The ultimate aim in studying prehistoric food remains is not only to establish how people obtained their food, but to reconstruct their actual diet as well. An overall picture of prehistoric diet requires, of course, constructing a comprehensive list of food resources available to the people and then answering such questions as these: What proportion of the diet was meat? How diverse were dietary sources? Did the principal diet sources change from season to season? Was food stored? These and many other questions can be answered only from composite pictures of prehistoric diet reconstructed from many sources of evidence.

Just occasionally, however, it is possible to gain insights into actual meals consumed thousands of years ago. The stomach of Tollund man, whose body was buried and preserved in a Danish peat bog, contained the remains of finely ground porridge made from barley, linseed, and several wild grasses (see Figure 5.2). No meat was found in his belly. Human droppings (coprolites or feces) found in dry caves in the United States and Mexico have been analyzed under fine microscopes. The inhabitants of *Lovelock Cave* in the central Nevada desert were eating bulrush and cattail seeds, as well as Lahontan chub from the waters of nearby Humboldt Lake. These fish were eaten raw or roasted over a fire. One coprolite contained the remains of at least fifty-one chub, calculated by a fish expert to represent a total fish weight of 3.65 pounds. The same people were eating adult and baby birds, as well as water tiger beetles. Human droppings from Texas caves near the mouth of the Pecos River have been subjected to pollen analyses so precise that the investigators established the sites to have been occupied regularly during the spring and summer months for thirteen hundred years between 800 B.C. and A.D. 550.

Although coprolite studies are a promising source of dietary information, the food remains from most sites are far too incomplete to allow more than a very general impression of diet. New research using the ratio between two stable carbon isotopes—carbon 12 and carbon 13 in animal tissue—enables scientists to establish the diet of prehistoric populations as they switch from wild foods to a predominantly maize diet, but the work is still in its infancy. Let us now look at some of the major sources of information on prehistoric subsistence surviving in archaeological sites.

## ANIMAL BONES

Broken animal bones can tell us a great deal about ancient hunting, herd management, and butchery practices. One can identify mammal species from their skeletal remains. Unfortunately, however, most animal bones found in archaeological sites are highly fragmentary. Until recently, archaeologists assumed that they were in such small fragments because the inhabitants slashed to ribbons every carcass they butchered. But researches on modern predator kills and controlled experiments on butchered animals, mainly in Africa, have shown that a great many complex and little-understood forces act on bones found in archaeological sites long after they are dropped where archaeologists find them. Weathering as bones decay in the open air, compaction of the sediments in which they are buried, chemistry of the soil, even treading by cattle or elephants can break up bones and help determine which parts of the body survive and which do not. Add to these accidents the butchering activities of the prehistoric inhabitants, and you have an archaeological jigsaw puzzle to unravel.

Generally speaking, the older the archaeological site, the more daunting it is to study postdepositional forces. The problem is particularly confusing at locations like *Olduvai Gorge* or *Koobi Fora* in East Africa, where hominids chewed and cut bones more than 1.75 million years ago—and probably scavenged their meat from predator kills into the bargain. On more recent sites, one finds that people utilized the carcasses they butchered to the maximum. Every piece of usable meat is stripped by the inhabitants from the bones of even the smallest animals or the portions of larger mammals brought back to the settlement. Sinews are made into thongs. Skins become clothing, containers, or even part of a shelter. Even the entrails are eaten. The hunters smash the bones themselves to get at the marrow or for manufacture into arrowheads or other tools. Animal bones are fragmented by many domestic activities, quite apart from trampling underfoot and scavenging by dogs and carnivores. Thus, the archaeologist is faced with the formidable task of identifying from tiny, discarded fragments the animal that was hunted or kept by the site's inhabitants. Further, the role the animal played in the economy, diet, and culture of the community must be assessed.

## Animal Bone Analysis (Zooarchaeology)

Most animal bone collections consist of thousands of scattered fragments from all parts of a site. Occasionally, however, a kill site, as in prehistoric bison kills on the Great Plains or the big game carcasses slaughtered by Stone Age hunters in East Africa, provides a chance to reconstruct the hunters' activities in more detail. Apart from such unusual finds, most collections have to be sorted out in the laboratory simply to give a general impression of hunting and stock-raising techniques at the site.

**Zooarchaeology** is the study of animal bones found in the archaeological record. Its goal is to reconstruct the environment and behavior of ancient peoples as thoroughly as animal remains allow. But the study of such bones is complicated by the natural and humanly induced processes that operate on organic remains as they lie on or in the ground. The study of this transition by animal remains from the biosphere to the lithosphere is known as **taphonomy**.

Taphonomy involves two related forms of research: observing recently dead carcasses as they are gradually transformed into fossils, and studying fossil remains with the knowledge gained from these observations. The crux of the zooarchaeologists' difficulty is their subject: a collection of animal bones, the part of the fossil assemblage that is actually excavated or collected. This fossil assemblage in turn consists of the body parts that survive in the archaeological record, an assemblage very different from the original community of live animals that once populated the natural environment in their "natural" proportions. Animal bone analysis involves two fundamental problems: (1) estimating the characteristics of a fossil assemblage from a collected sample, a statistical problem, and (2) a taphonomic problem, inferring what the original bone assemblage was like before it became a fossil one.

The first stage in bone analysis is to isolate the diagnostic fragments. Often only a few bones are identifiable to the species level. One three-thousand-year-old central African hunting camp yielded only 2,128 identifiable fragments out of 195,415 bones! The actual identifications are made by comparing such diagnostic body parts as teeth, jaws, horns, and some limb bones with modern animal skeletons (Figure 8.2). This procedure is not as easy as it sounds. Domestic sheep and goats have skeletons that are almost identical to those of their wild ancestors; the bones of the domestic ox closely resemble those of the African buffalo; and so on. But accurate

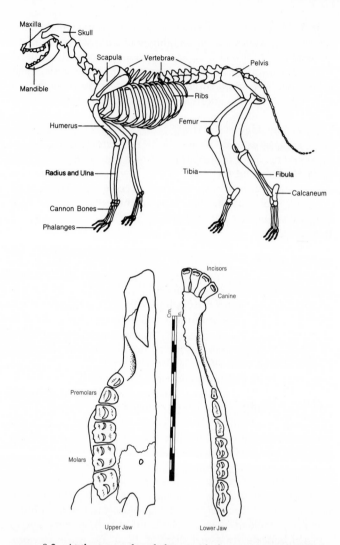

FIGURE 8.2    At the top, a dog skeleton with the most important body parts labeled from the bone identification point of view. At the bottom, a domestic ox jaw seen from below (upper jaw) and above (lower). Notice the characteristic cusp patterns of molars and premolars that grow in as the beast gets older.

identifications are vital, for they provide answers to many questions. Are both domestic and wild animals present? If so, what are the proportions of each group? Were the inhabitants concentrating on one species to the exclusion of all others? Are any now-extinct species present?

## Comparing Bone Collections

Having identified the animals present, how do you compare the proportions of different species from one site to those from another? The work is fraught with difficulty, because it is almost impossible to infer the once-living population from the surviving bones. Zooarchaeologists therefore apply two measures of specimen abundance to study the relative abundance of species:

*The number of Identified Specimens (NISP)* is a count of the number of bones or bone fragments. This assay has obvious disadvantages, because it is easy to overestimate one species at the expense of another, especially if its bones are cut into small fragments. The NISP has some limited use in conjunction with:

*The Minimum Number of Individuals (MNI),* a count of the number of individuals necessary to account for all the identifiable bones. This count is based on careful inventories of such individual body parts as, say, jaws. The MNI is a much more accurate estimate of the number of animals present in a collection.

Using these two counts together brackets the actual number of animals present in a bone sample, but the figure is still but an approximation, even when used with sophisticated computer programs.

## Species Abundance and Cultural Change

Climatic change rather than human culture was probably responsible for most long-term shifts in abundance of animal species during the great Ice Age. Some changes in the abundance of animals in bone collections, however, must reflect human activity—changes in the way in which people exploited other animals.

Zooarchaeologist Richard Klein has studied two coastal caves in South Africa to document such changes. The Klasies River cave on the Cape coast was occupied by "Middle Stone Age" hunters from about 130,000 to about 70,000 years ago, during a period of progressively colder climate. The people took seals, penguins, and shellfish and lived off the eland, a large antelope. The nearby Nelson's Bay cave was occupied by "Late Stone Age" people, after 20,000 years ago. These people took not only dangerous or elusive land mammals such as the Cape Buffalo, but birds and fish as well, both quarries requiring some skill to hunt or take successfully.

Did these changes between the two sites reflect cultural change or climatic differences? Were eland more abundant in earlier times, or just easier to hunt? Klein examined the toolkits from each cave, and found that Middle Stone Age artifacts were large and relatively crude, but the later Nelson's Bay people used bows, arrows, and an elaborate toolkit of small, more specialized tools. This more sophisticated toolkit allowed the Nelson's Bay groups to hunt more dangerous and tricky quarry with great success. Therefore, eland were less plentiful later not because of climatic change, but because other animals were hunted, too. Then too, in later times the population was larger. Klein suggests the growth from his examination of the limpet and tortoise shells from both sites. The Nelson's Bay specimens are smaller, as if these creatures were allowed to grow larger in earlier millennia when fewer people were there to exploit them.

## Game Animals

A collection of game animals yields a wealth of information about the great variety of mammals that ancient hunters killed with astonishingly simple weapons. North American Paleo-Indian bands used game drives, spears, and other weapons to hunt herds of now-extinct big game. So effective were early American hunters that some zoologists believe much Plains big game to have become extinct at least partly as a result of overhunting. Twenty thousand years ago, big-game hunters on the banks of the Dnieper and Don rivers in western Russia cooperated in pursuing mammoth and other arctic mammals. They cached supplies of game meat to tide them through the long, bitterly cold winters, which lasted more than eight months.

When the identified game animal bones are counted, one species may appear to dominate the collection. Some hunters concentrate on one or a few species, whether from economic necessity, convenience, or cultural preference. But the dominance can be misleading, for many societies restrict the hunting of particular animals. Others forbid males or females to eat certain species, though others may be consumed by everyone. The !Kung San of the Kalahari today have complicated personal and age- or sex-specific taboos to regulate their eating habits. No one may eat all the twenty-nine game animals regularly taken by the San. Indeed, no two individuals will have the same set of taboos. Such complicated restrictions are repeated with innumerable variations in other hunter-gatherer societies. The simple dietary figure of, say, 40 percent white-tailed deer and 20 percent wild geese may, in fact, reflect much more complex behavioral variables than mere concentration on two species.

### Domesticated Animals

Domestic animal bones present even more difficulties. Owners can affect their herds and flocks in many ways—by selective breeding to improve meat yields or to increase wool production, and by regulating the ages at which they slaughter surplus males and old animals. All domesticated animals originated from wild species with an inclination to be sociable, a characteristic that aided close association with humans. Animal domestication may have begun when a growing human population needed a regular food supply to support a greater density of people per square mile. Wild animals lack many characteristics valuable in their domestic relatives. Wild sheep have hairy coats, but their wool is unsuitable for spinning. The ancestors of oxen and domestic goats produced milk for their young, but not enough for human consumption. People have bred wild animals selectively for long periods to enhance special characteristics. Often the resulting domestic animals can no longer survive in the wild.

The history of domestic animals has to be written from fragmentary animal bones found in sites occupied by prehistoric farmers. The difference between domestic and wild animal bones is often so small that it may be next to impossible to tell the two apart. No one can tell a domestic sheep or goat from a wild one from a single jaw. One has to work with large numbers of animals, studying changing body sizes as the animals undergo selective breeding. Early Near Eastern sheep, are smaller and display less variation in size than their wild relatives. Even then it is, say the Scriptures, "difficult to tell the sheep from the goats."

## Aging and Butchery

Prehistoric peoples hunted game animals for food, used their hides for garments and tents, and their stomachs for bags. Domesticated animals provided meat and were used for plowing, riding, or for their milk. Establishing such practices from fragmentary animal bones is difficult, involving close study of both the age of slaughtered animals and the ways in which they were butchered.

Just as with comparing different assemblages, the problem is turning figures and percentages into meaningful interpretations of human behavior. Researches such as Lewis Binford's studies of Alaskan caribou hunters have provided valuable information for such approaches (see Chapter 10).

Determining the sex and age of an animal may provide a way of studying the hunting or stock-raising habits of those who slaughtered it. Many mammal species vary considerably in size and build between male and female. Consider the female human pelvis, which is shaped to accommodate the birth canal. With species such as the North American bison, you can often distinguish male from female by bone sizes, but the problem is much harder with animals where the size difference is less.

Teeth and the epiphyses (joints) at the end of limb bones are most commonly used to establish the ages of prehistoric animals. In almost all mammals, the epiphyses fuse to the limb bones at adulthood, and so one can immediately establish two categories of animals: immature and fully grown. Teeth and complete jaws are a more accurate way of establishing animal age. Teeth provide an almost continuous guide to the age of an animal from birth to old age. With complete

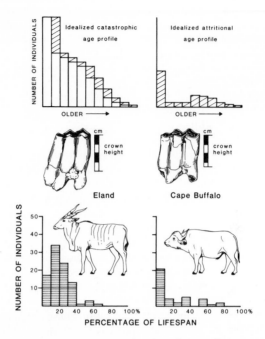

FIGURE 8.3 Idealized mortality data based on molar crowns of two common South African mammals, the eland and the Cape buffalo. (a) Idealized catastrophic age profile. (b) Idealized attritional age profile (for explanation, see text).

jaws one can study immature teeth as they erupt. Large numbers of them enable you to count with some accuracy the proportions of immature and very old animals with heavily worn teeth.

Richard Klein has used the height of tooth crowns to study the age of mammals taken by Stone Age hunters at Klasies River and Nelson's Bay caves in South Africa. He identified two "mortality distributions" that apply to prehistoric and living animal populations:

*A catastrophic age profile* is stable in size and structure, and has progressively fewer older individuals. This is the normal distribution for living antelope populations (Figure 8.3[a]).

If a group of hunters drives a herd over a cliff, you will find a distribution like this, for they are not being discriminating in their hunting.

*An attritional age profile* shows underrepresentation of prime-age animals relative to their abundance in living populations, but young and old are overrepresented. This profile is thought to result from scavenging or simple spear hunting (Figure 8.3[b]).

The eland tooth profiles at both Klasies River and Nelson's Bay were close to the catastrophic profile, and so Klein argued that they were hunted in mass game drives. In contrast, the more formidable Cape buffalo displayed an attritional profile, as if the hunters had preyed on immature and old beasts over long periods.

These interpretations are fine at a general level, but it is much harder to draw more specific conclusions. Lewis Binford's Nunamiut caribou hunters from Alaska direct much of their hunting activities toward obtaining meat for winter consumption. In the fall, they pursue caribou calves to obtain clothing. The heads and tongues of these young animals provide meat for the people who process the skins.

The fragmentary bones in an occupation level are the end product of the killing, cutting up, and consumption of domestic or wild animals. To understand the butchery process, the articulation of animal bones must be examined in the levels where they are found, or a close study made of fragmentary pieces. Rarely is an entire kill site preserved, like the famed Olsen-Chubbuck bison kill in Colorado, where more than 150 bison were driven to their death, then dismembered, more than 8,000 years ago. Archaeologist Joe Ben Wheat showed that for several days the hunters camped by their prey as they dismembered the uppermost bison in the confused heap of dead animals before them. When they had eaten their fill and dried enough meat to last them a month or more, they simply walked away and left the rotting carcasses. Archaeologists found the articulated and butchered skeletons thousands of years later.

Interpreting butchery techniques is a complicated matter, for many variables affect the way in which the carcass is dismembered. Toughness of hide, tools available, size and portability of the animal, and potential use for skins, even horn, a few of the variables. The only way to interpret body parts in this context is by understanding in detail the cultural system that generated them. The herders, finding a constant surplus óf males beyond their breeding requirements, may castrate some of these animals and then use them for riding and dragging carts or plows. But even with some insights into the cultural system and excellent bone preservation, it is hard to interpret the meaning of butchering techniques.

So many factors affect the counts of identified bones from any collection of animal remains that one has to interpret the fragments in the context of artifact patterns, site formation processes, and all other sources of data potentially bearing on the behavior of the people who killed the animals.

## VEGETABLE REMAINS

Gathering and agriculture are almost invariably unrepresented in most sites, because the tiny seeds and other vegetable remnants that result from such activities as food storage, grinding, and harvesting are among the most fragile of all archaeological remains. Except for occasional burned seeds found in hearths or storage pits, the vegetable remains from human feces, and grain impressions in clay pot walls, almost all evidence for prehistoric gathering and agriculture comes from dry sites, where preservation conditions are almost perfect (Figure 8.4).

Recovering such fragile remains requires slow work with fine screens. Some archaeologists have started to use flotation methods to recover thousands of hitherto unrecoverable vegetable remains. With this technique, water or chemicals are used to free tiny seeds from the deposits. The freshly excavated earth is poured into a container and sinks slowly to the bottom while the light seeds float on the surface. Stuart Struever was able to recover 36,000 hickory nut fragments, 4,200 acorn shells, and 2,000 seeds from other species from ovens, hearths, and pits in the *Apple Creek* site in the lower Illinois Valley using simple flotation techniques. At the *Ali Kosh* mound in Iran, Kent Flannery and Frank Hole thought that plant remains were scarce at the site. Then they used

FIGURE 8.4  A grain impression preserved on a clay pot fragment
from an early farming site in eastern England. (Approximately 2.2
inches.)

flotation methods and recovered 40,000 seeds from their
trenches. Flotation methods have begun to revolutionize the
study of plant remains, for they provide large seed samples
that can be studied with statistical methods.

Most of our knowledge of such early major food crops as
wheat, barley, and maize has so far come from dry caves
rather than flotation. Richard MacNeish assembled a continuous sequence of human occupation for the period 10,000
years ago to the Spanish Conquest from *Tehuacán* Valley in
Mexico. He dug more than a dozen open sites and caves, all
so dry that they yielded 80,000 wild plant remains and 25,000

specimens of domestic corn. When the vegetable remains had been identified, MacNeish knew that the inhabitants of Tehuacán were getting 18 percent of their food from cultivation of corn and other crops in 5000 B.C., and a third of it from agriculture in 3400 B.C. Fifteen hundred years later, several hybrid varieties of maize were in use and agriculture was far more important than foraging for wild plants. He also found that the earliest maize cobs, dating to around 5000 B.C. and earlier, were no more than 0.78 inch long, but later ones were far larger. Unfortunately, MacNeish was unable to identify the original wild ancestor of Tehuacán maize, probably the native grass *teosinte*.

Farmers modify the landscape around them by grazing their herds and by clearing forests. Simple, shifting cultivation techniques required new garden acreage every season. Each time cultivation required more cleared woodland, drastic environmental changes have been triggered. Few people have ever tried to assess how profoundly early agricultural economies affected the world environment. Danish botanist Johannes Iversen was able to spot a sharp drop in the percentages of tree pollens in layers of northern European peat bogs dating to about 3000 B.C. The forest trees declined suddenly. At the same time, the number of grass pollens increased sharply. Traces of several cultivation weeds also appeared at the same time. Iversen was able to pin down the moment when farmers first cleared natural forest to make way for their crops.

This early clearance activity dramatizes how very little we know about prehistoric agriculture and gathering, simply because the archaeological evidence is so hard to recover. Our ignorance has led to the belief that all hunter-gatherers spent their lives in a perennial state of starvation, relieved occasionally by meat-eating orgies. Nothing could be further from the truth. The !Kung San, present-day inhabitants of the Kalahari Desert in southern Africa, know of at least eighty-five edible seeds and roots. Most of the time they eat but eight of these. The rest of the vegetable resource base provides a reliable cushion for this foraging population in times when key vegetable foods are scarce. Such people have a buffer against famine that many farmers with their cleared lands, much higher population densities, and crops that rely on regular rainfall rarely enjoy. Is a farming life really to be preferred? Our glimpses into prehistory suggest this tantalizing question.

## BIRDS, FISH, AND MOLLUSKS

Bird bones, although very informative, are often neglected at the expense of larger mammal remains. In 1926, Hildegarde Howard studied a large bird bone collection from an Indian midden on the eastern shores of San Francisco Bay. The inhabitants had hunted many water birds, especially ducks, geese, and cormorants. When Howard looked more closely at the bones, she found that all the geese were migrant winter visitors, which frequent the bay area between January and April. Nearly all the cormorants were immature specimens, birds about five to six weeks old. Had the Indians been raiding cormorant rookeries? Howard consulted rookery records and estimated that the birds had been killed about June 28. Thus, the site had been occupied both during the winter and early summer, one of many settlements where bird bones give evidence of seasonal occupation.

Fishing, like bird hunting, became more important as people began to specialize in different lifeways and adapt to highly specific environments. Evidence for fishing comes both from artifacts and from fragile fish bones, which, when they survive, can be identified with considerable accuracy.

Freshwater and ocean fish may be caught with nets or with basketlike fish traps. Indians who lived on the site of modern Boston in about 2500 B.C. built a dam of vertical stakes and brush. When the Atlantic tides rose, fish were directed into gaps in the dam and trapped in huge numbers. Barbed fish spears and fish hooks are relatively common finds in some archaeological sites, but such artifacts tell us little about the weight of fishing in prehistoric subsistence. Did the people fish all year, or only when salmon were running? Did they concentrate on coastal species or venture far offshore in large canoes? Such questions can be answered only by examining the fish bones themselves.

The Chumash Indians of southern California were remarkably skillful fishermen, who went far offshore in frameless plank canoes to fish with hook and line, basket, net, and harpoon. It was no surprise when the fish bones found on archaeological sites at Century Ranch, Los Angeles, included not only the bones of shallow-water fish like the leopard shark and California halibut, but the remains of albacore, ocean skipjack, and large rock fish, species that occur in deep water and can be caught only there. Without the fish bones, no one would have had any idea how effective the maritime adaptation of the Chumash and related groups was. Early Spanish accounts speak of more than ten thousand Indians living in the Santa Barbara area of California alone, a large population indeed. Archaeology has shown that this maritime population was able to exploit a very broad spectrum of marine resources.

Fishing, with its relatively predictable food resources and high protein potential, allows much more sedentary settlement than other forms of hunting and gathering. The Northwest Coast Indians enjoyed a very rich maritime culture, based on ocean fishing and salmon runs that enabled large numbers of people to live in one area for long periods.

Shellfish from seashore, lake, or river supplied a good portion of the prehistoric diet for many thousands of years. Freshwater mollusks were important both to California Indians and to prehistoric people living in the southeastern United States. Most mollusks have limited food value in themselves, and so great quantities are needed to feed even a few people. One estimate for a hundred peoples' mollusk needs for a month runs as high as three tons. In all probability, mollusks were more a supplemental food at set times of the year than a staple. They were simply too much effort to collect in sufficient quantity.

Even sporadic collecting led to rapidly accumulating piles of shells **(shell middens)** at strategic points on lake or ocean shores, near rocky outcrops or tidal pools where mollusks were commonly found.

Shell midden excavations in California and elsewhere have yielded thousands of shells, which are counted, identified, and also measured to check for size changes. When Claude Warren sampled a shell midden near San Diego, California, he found five major species of shellfish commonly exploited by the inhabitants. The earliest shellfish collectors concentrated on the bay mussel and oysters, both of which flourish on rocky shores. But, by 4000 b.c., the lagoon by the shell middens had so silted up that sand-loving scallops and Venus shells were now collected, for the earlier species were unable to flourish in the new, sandy environment. Soon afterward, however, the lagoon became clogged and the shellfish collectors moved away, never to return. And their abandoned seashells told the story of the changing environment around the sites.

Both fresh and saltwater shells were widely used as prehistoric ornaments. Gulf Coast shells were bartered over enormous distances of the southeastern and midwestern United States, to peoples who had never seen the ocean. Sometimes such ornaments could assume incredible prestige value. When nineteenth-century explorer David Livingstone visited Chief Shinte in central Africa in 1855, he found him wearing two seashells that had come a thousand miles inland from the distant East African coast. The chief told him that two such shells would buy a slave, five a large ivory elephant tusk. Small wonder that enterprising merchants were trading china replicas of these shells in central Africa half a century later.

## ROCK ART

Sometimes prehistoric rock art gives vivid insight into subsistence activities of long ago, into hunts and fishing expeditions in the distant past. Hunter-gatherers and fishermen have left paintings of their daily life behind on the walls of caves and rockshelters. Careful examination of these paintings can take one back centuries and millennia to the time when the people were killing the animals whose bones lie in occupation deposits under the observer's feet. Many details of weapons, of domestic equipment, and of hunting and fishing methods can be discerned in these vivid scenes.

The Stone Age paintings of southern Africa have long been known for their depictions of life in prehistoric times. At Tsoelike River rockshelter in Lesotho, southern Africa, fishermen are depicted assembled in their boats (Figure 8.5). They have cornered a shoal of fish that are swimming around

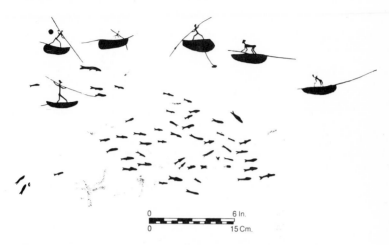

FIGURE 8.5 The fishing scene from Tsoelike rockshelter, Lesotho, southern Africa.

in confusion. Some boats have lines that seem to be anchors. The fishermen are busy spearing their quarry. Another famed scene depicts a peacefully grazing herd of ostriches. Among them lurks a hunter wearing an ostrich skin, his legs and bow protruding beneath the belly of the apparently harmless bird. One wonders if his hunt was successful.

The artists painted big game hunts, honey collectors, women gathering fruit, cattle raids, even red-coated British soldiers. Scenes like these take one back to hot days when a small group of hunters pursued their wounded quarry until it weakened and collapsed. The painting hunters, having stalked their prey for hours, relax in the shade as they watch its death throes. Then they settle down to butcher the dead animal before carrying the meat and skin home to be shared with their group. Few artifacts survive from scenes such as these. But the objective of reconstructing ancient subsistence patterns is to re-create, from the few patterned traces that have survived in the soil, just such long days in the sun.

# 9

## INTERACTION

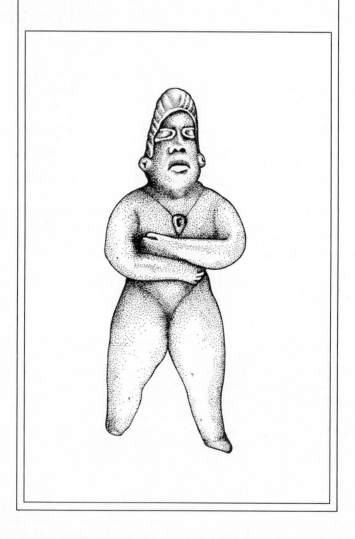

> Thus the sum of things is ever being replenished,
> and mortals live one and all by give and take. Some
> races wax and wane, and in a short space the tribes
> of living things are changed and like runners hand
> on the torch of life.
>
> LUCRETIUS, *De Rerum Natura*

The toolkits and food remains found in archaeological sites reflect their inhabitants' material culture and subsistence activities. Hunter-gatherers tend to have portable toolkits, manufactured for the most part from organic materials that do not survive well in archaeological sites (see Figure 4.5). Many of their sites are temporary camps. Rarely can the archaeologist look at the patterning of artifacts and food remains in such camps, for many are gone forever. But the more sedentary farmer settles much longer in one spot and is confronted with much more elaborate annual tasks. The farmer has to store each year's food surplus, too, an activity that immediately adds complexity to a farming settlement. Substantial houses, storage pits, cemeteries, threshing floors, cattle enclosures—all these can be elements in even a small farming village.

Archaeologists study patterning in such structures as houses and storage pits just as thoroughly as they study artifacts and food remains. They also study distributions in time and space of different communities and relationships between them. All these activities are classified as **settlement archaeology**, which reveals the many ways in which individual communities relate to one another—through, among many, trade, religious beliefs, and social ties.

## SETTLEMENT PATTERNS

Settlement patterns are determined by many factors, including environment, economic practices, and technological skills. The distribution of San camps in the Kalahari Desert depends on the availability of water supplies and vegetable foods. Ancient Maya settlements in Mexico were laid out in a pattern determined by political and religious organization. Village layout can be determined by the need to protect cattle against lions or raiding parties. Other settlements may be strung out at intervals along a vital trade route, perhaps a river. Population growth or increases in herd size may overtax the capacity of hunting grounds or grazing areas, leading to new adaptations and alterations in the settlement pattern. Even the positions of houses are dictated by complex and various social, economic, and personal factors that may defy explanation—especially when one has only archaeological evidence to go on.

Settlement archaeology is part of the analysis of human interactions with, and adaptations to, the natural and social environment. The houses and villages of a prehistoric society, like the artifacts and food residues by their hearths, are part of the settlement pattern. This pattern involves relationships among people who decided—for practical, political, economic, ideological, and social reasons—to place their houses, settlements, and religious structures where they did. By studying settlement patterns, we have a chance to examine the intangible factors that caused culture change in prehistory.

Canadian archaeologist Bruce Trigger has recognized three distinct levels of human settlement. The first is the single building; the second, the arrangement of such buildings within a community; the third, the distribution of communities against the landscape. We will examine each of these three levels briefly.

### Structures

Human structures are of infinite variety, all the way from the simple brush shelters of hunter-gatherers to the elaborate villas of Imperial Rome. The pyramids of Giza, Maya temples, even cattle pens, are all structures. Both environmental and societal factors, as well as economic considerations, have dictated the design of human structures. Twenty thousand years ago big game hunters on the West Russian plains lived half underground in houses made of skins and mammoth (arctic elephant) bones. These structures were effective in protecting their inhabitants against cold in a timberless environment. In contrast, tropical African farmers live where daytime temperatures regularly exceed 100 degrees Fahrenheit and the nights too are hot. And so they live much of their lives in the shade of their pole-and-mud huts, whose thatched roofs project far beyond the walls. Grass, puddled mud, and other convenient local raw materials provide insulation for humankind—whether from summer's heat or arctic cold.

Details of house design are often determined by social and economic considerations. Many societies have had standardized house plans, for everyone had the same economic opportunities and the same amount of wealth. The householders carried out various activities at home, reflected in the patterning of artifacts in abandoned rooms. Variations in artifact content can reflect different subsistence activities, social status, wealth, and manufacturing skills.

When Kent Flannery and his students excavated farming villages in the Valley of Oaxaca, Mexico, dating to between 1350 and 850 b.c., they not only uncovered and recorded the one-room, thatched, pole-and-mud-houses, but plotted the associated artifact patterns as well. They distinguished carefully between the house with its contents and the cluster of household storage pits, graves, and garbage heaps that lay nearby. Flannery plotted household features very carefully, and he also identified areas where special activites took place from the specialist toolkits—for bead making and the like—associated with them. Every household obtained, processed, and stored food, though the types of food consumed by each varied, and some Oaxacan households spent much time making stone tools or ornaments. These specialist activities presumably supplied the needs of the community as a whole. In this Mexican example, and in all studies of individual structures, the artifacts and activites associated with them are just as important to the archaeologist as the design and layout of the structure itself.

## Communities

Every household member interacts with other members of the household and also with individuals in other households within the community. And entire households interact with other households as well. Once one begins to look at a community of households, new complexities enter the picture. The first is permanency of settlement, which is affected primarily by the realities of subsistence and ecology. How long San camps are occupied is determined by availability of water, game, and vegetable foods near the site; the camp moves at regular intervals. At the other extreme, early city dwellers in Mesopotamia who used irrigation in their fields never had to move their settlement.

The layout of a community is greatly determined by social and political factors, particularly by family and kinship ties. Marriage customs and rules of residence and inheritance may multiply the number of houses associated wtih one household. A father may live with his sons in a cattle camp and their families occupy houses within his enclosure. Variables such as land ownership may be reflected in community layout, too. The only way archaeologists can study these factors is by looking for patterns of settlement features and artifacts that may reflect kin groups and other social ties.

The largest community settlement pattern ever investigated systematically is that of *Teotihuacán,* where René Millon has mapped dozens of residential compounds, a market, and vast ceremonial structures (Figure 9.1). He even found a special quarter where foreigners from Oaxaca—revealed by their distinctive pottery—lived in an alien city for centuries. Millon sought the answers to many questions. What social classes existed in the city? What specialist crafts were practiced and where? How many people lived at Teotihuacán at different periods? The only way to answer such questions was to map the entire city and make comprehensive surface collections and test excavations to give an overall picture of the total settlement pattern.

How can one measure the size of small villages, let alone huge cities like Teotihuacán? Informed guesses are sometimes

FIGURE 9.1 Teotihuacán, Valley of Mexico, a prehistoric city that was mapped in detail by René Millon. The Pyramid of the Moon is in the foreground; the Avenue of the Dead stretches into the distance; the giant Pyramid of the Sun is to the left of the avenue in the distance. From *Urbanization at Teotihuacán, Mexico*, v.1, pt.1, *The Teotihuacán Map: Text* by René Millon, copyright © 1973 by René Millon, by permission of the author.

useful, but the only reliable method is to calculate the population by the number of households in a village at a given moment in its history. And such calculations require large-scale excavations and complex statistical tests. In Teotihuacán, Millon counted rooms and possible sleeping spaces and came up with an intelligent guess of one hundred and twenty-five thousand—a conservative estimate.

If a village is growing, there comes a time when it can grow no further. Some people then form a new settlement that flourishes alongside the original village. But sometimes, as in Oaxaca, the villagers continued to live in a steadily growing settlement. Eventually it outgrew its contemporary neighbors. Why did the villagers elect to stay together? Did the larger site survive because its location was favorable for trade or religious ceremonies? These are the sorts of questions that archaeologists can answer only by looking at the site distributions and the resources in their surrounding natural environments. A community does not exist in isolation.

## Catchment Areas

A century ago, geographers studying European agriculture formed the notion of catchment areas, a zone of natural resources around a settlement upon which it can draw. The farther the resources in an area are from a community, the less likely they are to be exploited. Anthropologist Richard Lee found that !Kung San women are unlikely to forage more than a comfortable day's walk from their camp. The camp thus has a five-mile-radius catchment area for foraging, although, of course, the terrain will not necesarily be uniform enough for it to be circular.

Catchment areas are a useful concept in archaeology, especially in studying hunters and gatherers, people who move about over extensive areas and use a number of campsites during the year. **Site catchment analysis** has become popular in recent years as a way of making empirical statements about the sources of materials recovered in archaeological sites. The two key concepts in this type of settlement archaeology are:

*The economic catchment area* of a site is the territory from which the food resources consumed by the site's inhabitants are obtained. Such areas vary in size and shape according to the resources exploited, the function of the site, and the lifeway of the inhabitants. Clearly, the accuracy with which the economic catchment can be defined will depend on the precision with which one can identify food remains in the site itself.

*The site exploitation territory* is quite different, a theoretical statement about the area around a site. This land is *assumed* to have been used regularly for subsistence by its inhabi-

tants. The boundary of this theoretical territory is defined
by using "least-cost" principles—maximum radii of travel
that people will cover on foot. Two hours' walking time is
about 6.2 miles (10 km). Much depends on the type of resources and how they are exploited. Much smaller radii,
say 0.6 mile (1 km), are useful when analyzing farming
economies, where the land is exploited very intensively,
for it is most labor- and land-intensive to use land close to
the village. The boundaries of such radii are based on as-
sumptions about normal human behavior, and on examining the economic potential of resources lying within
them. Thus, this type of site catchment analysis is little
more than a statement about resources that were potentially available to the site's inhabitants.

Site catchment analysis involves examining both the economic catchment and the site exploitation territory, as a way
of assessing the relationship between all that was *potentially*
available in the environment and that which was *actually* exploited. Typically, variations in the economic potential of a
site catchment area are compared with variations on patterns
of data from the site itself.

Site catchment analysis helps with a major problem in settlement archaeology: defining variations in activities at different sites, and testing hypotheses about how sites were
linked. The latter task is especially needed when studying
prehistoric hunting and foraging territories and early trade.

One good example of site catchment analysis comes from
highland Mexico. Kent Flannery examined the resources he
found in excavations at San José Mogote in Oaxaca (1150–850
B.C.). By taking the many seeds found by flotation techniques, the animal bones, mineral resources such as clay and
salt, and imported objects including seashells, he found that
San José Mogote needed a radius of less than one to three
miles to satisfy its basic agricultural needs. Today common
minerals and seasonal wild vegetable foods are found within
the three-mile circle, game meat and construction material
within the nine-mile zone. Exotic trade materials and the requirements of ceremonial life required occasional collecting
trips up to thirty miles from the settlement, and some contacts over longer distances. When Flannery plotted the catch-

ment areas of neighboring villages, he found that the one- to three-mile circles of each settlement did not overlap, but the wider ones, where minerals and other needs were satisfied, did (Figure 9.2). Seasonal camps were built in the outer zones, where every community shared resources.

## Site Interactions and Distributions

Site catchment analysis is really a form of resource inventory, but one that leads us to explore the interactions between communities. No human being has ever lived in complete isolation, for even the smallest hunter-gatherer family group has at least fleeting contacts with neighboring bands at certain times of the year. But, as human societies become more complex and settlements more lasting, intercommunity relationships become much more complicated. Different settlements depend more and more on one another for essential raw materials (salt or copper ore), and for specialist products (stone knives, religious ornaments, and the like). Growing villages might split into two settlements that, though separated in space, still maintain close ties of kinship. Human settlement patterns are not just site dots on maps. They are complex and constantly changing networks of human interaction, of trade, religion, and social ties, of differing adaptations to local environmental challenges.

Archaeologists study settlement patterns on this scale by plotting their data on site distribution maps derived from field surveys and aerial photographs. Their ultimate goal is to reconstruct the factors that caused the settlement pattern—now a collection of site dots—in the first place. Of course, any attempt to use a distribution map involves trying to assess the reliability of the data on the map. Do the painstakingly collected data reflect human actions of the past or merely earnest guesswork by archaeologists? The analysis of distributions and settlement patterns comes under the general heading of **spatial analysis**.

## Site Hierarchies

Spatial analysis in archaeology begins as we carefully draw a classification of archaeological sites in a region, like that

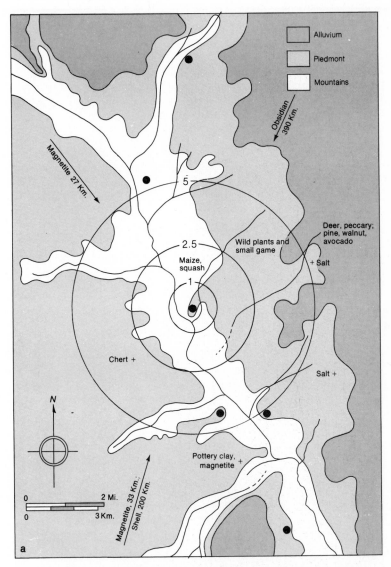

FIGURE 9.2  (a) Site catchment area around San José Mogote, Valley of Oaxaca. (b, following page) The overlapping catchment zones of villages in the same area. (Radii in kilometers.)

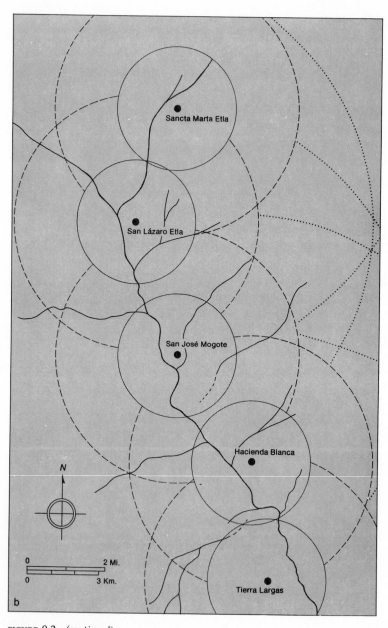

FIGURE 9.2  *(continued)*

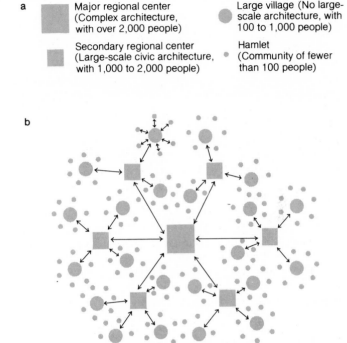

**a**

Major regional center
(Complex architecture,
with over 2,000 people)

Secondary regional center
(Large-scale civic architecture,
with 1,000 to 2,000 people)

Large village (No large-
scale architecture, with
100 to 1,000 people)

Hamlet
(Community of fewer
than 100 people)

**b**

FIGURE 9.3   A site hierarchy in Mesoamerica. (a) Simplified hierarchy of site types. (b) Hypothetical site hierarchy on the ground, with the major regional center serving secondary centers spaced at regular intervals. These in turn serve larger villages and their networks of hamlets.

done by archaeologists working in the Valley of Mexico (Figure 9.3). Each of these site types has a relationship to others, the total distribution of all site types making up a settlement pattern. Each site type is defined by the characteristic structures, artifact patterns, and forms in it. These definitions provide us with a way to organize the sites into a hierarchy of successive levels of settlements. We then need to look at the processes by which the hierarchy arose in the first place.

# TRADE

Human subsistence is based on exploiting the natural environment. Many hunter-gatherer societies were self-sufficient in their dietary needs. They used only the raw materials within their regular territory. But many societies, especially after the invention of agriculture, were no longer self-sufficient. They needed access to a much wider range of raw materials and finished artifacts, many of which they obtained by trading with neighboring communities.

Much prehistoric trade took the form of simple exchange, often by offering an object to a trading partner on the assumption that a return gift would be given at some future date. This form of trade is common in New Guinea and the Pacific today. The bartering of day-to-day items such as foodstuffs between villagers living in different environments was obviously conducted with one set of rules, and commodities accessible in shared catchment zones, such as obsidian (volcanic glass), were subject to quite different factors. Here, of course, the distance of a community from an obsidian source and the number of people requiring it may have set the pattern of exchange. Each community could barter communally for its raw materials, which might in turn be handed over to specialist craftspeople who produced the finished artifacts for others in the group.

Trade is generaly recognized in the archaeological record by exotic objects discovered in sites miles away from their point of origin. The Indians of the Lake Superior region obtained copper from natural outcrops near the lake. They traded the precious metal over thousands of miles, as far away as Florida. Perhaps the best-known trade commodity of all is obsidian, widely prized for making knives and shiny mirrors. Obsidian is found at a few localities in the Near East and at many more in Mesoamerica. In the Near East, it has been possible to identify the sources of the obsidian found in early farming villages by comparing the trace elements in raw obsidian from the source areas with that in traded artifacts. After dozens of sites had been examined, Colin Renfrew and other archaeologists concluded that villages spaced at regular intervals were passing about half the obsidian they received to their more distant neighbors, so that small supplies were carried over enormous distances. In Mesoamerica, obsidian was traded in regional networks through informal trading relationships that gradually became more and more organized as new local rulers began to control the valuable trade.

Trade, indeed, has been thought of as one variable that contributed to the origins of urban life and the increasing complexity of societies. Undoubtedly, trade became more complicated as social and political controls over raw materials and luxuries increased. This increased complexity may be reflected in the wider variety of exotic artifacts in individual sites.

But trade goods themselves are less important to archaeologists than the mechanisms that brought the goods to the site, and so archaeologists have followed economists and geographers in looking at trading mechanisms. All prehistoric trade involved at least two parties. There is no such thing as trade in general. Each commodity creates specific problems of trading, particularly in transportation. The motives for trading, too, are varied. People have traded for survival, for prestige, for religious reasons, and for wealth, among the many reasons. In more complex societies, the ruler and his or her followers generally control trade. They develop and police trade networks and employ specialist merchants and traders to keep it going.

Take the lowland Maya of Mesoamerica. They lived in a uniform, lowland rainforest environment that lacked rocks suitable for grinding maize, salt, obsidian, and many luxury materials. All these rocks could be obtained from the highlands and from the valley of Mexico, as well as from Guatemala and elsewhere. But the necessary trading networks and connections for obtaining these essentials had to be organized, not simply for individual communities but for the hundreds of lowland settlements with common assets, in an area where communication is very difficult. The Maya built complex trade networks through the authority of the major ceremonial centers and their leaders. Imports such as grinding stones and obsidian were exchanged down through the hierarchy of Maya settlements from the larger centers to smaller ones. These state-organized trade networks made the Maya communities very dependent on one another.

These Maya trade networks are being studied in artifact patterns at hundreds of sites and the distribution of exotic tools and materials through the Maya lowlands. But these studies are merely preliminaries to considering trade as one of many elements in prehistoric settlement patterns, one that linked households, communities, and regions into trade networks controlled and regulated by chiefs, religious leaders, or specialist merchants. Many of these controls can be understood only if we examine prehistoric religious beliefs and social organization.

## SOCIAL ORGANIZATION

Our old friend the cartoon archaeologist believed that you could never find out anything about peoples' social organization and religious beliefs from archaeological excavation. This truism is untrue. By studying artifact patterns and stylistic changes in material culture, one can gain some insights into prehistoric social organization.

Many anthropologists have defined several broad levels of sociocultural evolution in prehistory. These provide a general framework for tracing human social organization from the first simple family structures of the earliest humans to the highly complex state-organized societies of the early civilizations.

For most of prehistory, humanity flourished in **bands** of twenty-five to sixty people linked by kinship ties. This tightly knit organization encouraged cooperative hunting and gathering and sharing of resources. Then early farmers, with their more sedentary life, associated in groups of bands linked by kinship clans into **tribes**. All resources were owned by the tribe as a whole, and a tribal council would govern affairs. Among tribal societies in which different kin groups assumed some order of rank, **chiefdoms** formed. The leaders of these lineages coordinated management of food surpluses and distribution of specialist products. Their authority was often maintained by their spiritual power. **State-organized societies** developed out of chiefdoms. They were governed by a ruling class that headed a bureaucracy and governed through a justice system. The ownership of land and control of religion were in the leaders' hands. All society was ranked in social classes—warriors, traders, peasants, and so on. State-organized societies were the foundation of the earliest civilizations.

The archaeological evidence for social organization comes from several sources. Burials and their associated grave goods can give information on social ranking, which can be obtained by studying the possessions and ornaments deposited with each skeleton in a site. A most spectacular example comes from the royal cemetary at *Ur-of-the-Chaldees*, Mesopotamia. British archaeologist Leonard Woolley uncovered 1,850 graves, 16 of which stood out as special sepulchers because of their very rich grave furniture. The royal corpses were laid to rest in brick chambers accompanied by their personal attendants. The entire court and the royal bodyguard, complete with wagons and weapons, then lined up in order outside the burial chamber and lay down to die after taking poison. Woolley was able to describe the members of court, their order of precedence, and their distinctive costumes. All these corpses contrasted sharply with the hundreds of humbler burials elsewhere in the cemetery.

## ARTIFACT PATTERNING AND SETTLEMENT PATTERNS

When James Deetz studied the archaeology of the Arikara Indians of South Dakota, he used changes in pottery design as a means for examining alterations in social organization through time. He began by assuming that all the pots were made by women, and that mothers passed on styles to their daughters, as is often done in Indian societies. He assumed also that there would be continuity in pottery designs through time, with each household perpetuating its pot styles over many generations. Deetz then excavated an Arikara site that was known to date to between A.D. 1700 and 1780. He found three occupation zones, each with distinctive pottery styles. The wares from the earliest levels fit into well-defined classes. Clearly, the designers had definite ideas about what each type of vessel should like. But pottery in the two later occupations was much harder to classify, as if the closely knit cultural traditions of earlier generations had broken down. No tight clusterings of attributes were there to work with.

Deetz looked at contemporary historical records and found that the Arikara had moved up the Missouri more and more frequently between 1700 and 1800. A shortage of timber upstream caused them both to shift villages more often and to build smaller houses. When they moved into more open country, the men spent more and more time trading, acting as middlemen between white traders and Plains Indians. As farming became less important, female roles changed. Instead of living with their mothers, an arrangement that would lead to continuity in pottery styles, many women moved away to new villages. This change was reflected, Deetz concluded, in more variable pottery traditions and other changes in artifact patterning.

The Deetz study is a fascinating experiment in using artifacts to study social structure, one of many such attempts in recent years. The Arikara conclusions have been challenged on several grounds. The site Deetz dug was occupied at a time when the Arikara were in contact with many groups and when population was falling sharply. Could the less-patterned styles reflect a period of depopulation—perhaps another explanation for the breakdown of family pottery styles? Much more fieldwork will be needed before Deetz's pioneer conclusions are confirmed.

Many archaeologists assume that a direct relationship connects the degree to which people interacted with one another and the stylistic similarities of their pots and other artifacts. The problem is to test this assumption against the archaeological record. Unfortunately, few areas of the world have sufficient data to follow up on Deetz's pioneer attempt.

## RELIGIOUS BELIEFS

An anonymous archaeologist wrote cynically that "religion is the last resort of troubled archaeologists." At one time archaeologists were inclined to call any object they couldn't identify "ritual." Some still do. Obviously, some important sites were of religious significance. The Pyramid of the Sun at *Teotihuacán* is one, *Stonehenge* in England another. Some of

FIGURE 9.4   A Venus figurine head from Brassempouy, France.

the earliest religious objects in the world are the so-called
Venus figurines made in Europe twenty-five thousand years
ago (Figure 9.4).

Some evidence for religious rituals comes from burials. The
Neanderthal peoples of western Europe deliberately buried
their dead seventy thousand years ago with a variety of
goods. Hundreds of *Adena* and *Hopewell* burial mounds dot
the landscape of the Midwest, holding the graves of thousands of clan leaders and lesser personages, each buried with
distinctive grave furniture, some with elaborate cult objects.
The building of the Hopewell mounds was carried out step
by step, as the dead were deposited on an earthen platform

FIGURE 9.5   The Great Serpent Mound, built by the Adena people as a ceremonial earthwork.

that was later covered with a large mound. The famed Great Serpent Mound in Ohio is an Adena ceremonial earthwork, whose exact religious significance still escapes us (Figure 9.5).

Many more-complex prehistoric societies enjoyed highly organized religions that were reflected in widely distributed and mostly characteristic art styles. The *Olmec* art style of Mexico was carried over thousands of square miles of highlands and lowlands after 1000 B.C. Olmec art's snarling jaguar and human motifs coincide with distinctive religious beliefs that linked large and small communities all over Mexico.

Most societies' religious beliefs were interpreted and maintained through regular religious rituals conducted at specific times of the year, as at harvests and plantings. These regular ceremonies were vital to the elaborate organization of newly emerging complex societies. The predictable yearly round of religious life gave society an orderly framework for redistributing food, disposing of surplus cattle, accumulating wealth, and other economic functions. The long-term effects of these new, unifying religious beliefs were startling. Between 1150 and 850 B.C., Mesoamerican society began to undergo rapid transformation. Administrative and religious authority came together in the hands of leaders of a newly ranked society, with specialists and a hierarchy of settlements. This organization contrasted with the dispersed villages of earlier times. More elaborate public buildings appear, as temples and monumental buildings begin to reflect individual communities' common involvement in public works. In Mesoamerica and elsewhere, the ultimate sacred beliefs and rituals of a society are linked to the processes of social and environmental change that act upon it.

The only way in which we can hope to zero in on these types of fundamental beliefs is by looking at obvious religious artifacts and their patterning within archaeological sites. The close relationship between the spread of Mexican religious beliefs and the trading of fine art objects, new pottery forms, conch shells, and the sting-ray spines used in self-mutilation rites, we know of from painted murals. The distribution of such artifacts in areas away from the Olmec lowlands, and the distribution of the same imports within individual villages, in houses and public buildings, can give us some clues as to when the new beliefs first took hold over a wider area. By studying burials and artifact patternings, as well as the artifacts themselves, we can gain insight into how religious beliefs acted as one of the many variables affecting the ever-changing societies of prehistoric times.

In recent years, many researchers have turned to ethnohistorical and historical records to decipher prehistoric religious beliefs. Only a few years after the Spanish Conquest of Mexico, missionary Fray Bernardino de Sahagun (c. 1499–1590) laboriously recorded a mass of information about Aztec life and civilization from Indian survivors of the Conquest. In his great work, *A General History of the Things of New Spain,* he described not only early Aztec history, but minute details of Indian religion, even of Aztec philosophy and poetry. Modern scholars are interpreting his writings and discovering that Aztec religious beliefs were at least as sophisticated and complex as the Catholic beliefs that replaced them.

David Lewis-Williams is an expert on prehistoric rock art

in southern Africa, on an art tradition painted on the walls of caves and rockshelters for thousands of years until Europeans came. This art depicts animals, hunters during the chase, scenes of camp life, and religious ceremonies, as well as complex signs and symbols. No painters survived into this century, but Lewis-Williams dug into early descriptions of the paintings by Victorian investigators, who also recorded some of the San oral traditions about the paintings. His research has enabled him to evaluate some of the paintings of eland and other animals in their ancient symbolic context. The paintings were integral to the symbolic world of the San, a world intimately tied to the animals they hunted.

Recent advances in deciphering Maya hieroglyphs have enabled experts to see more deeply into ancient religion in the Mexican lowlands. Few Maya documents (codices) survived the Spanish Conquest, and so Francis Robicek and others have applied themselves to painted vases that accompanied the dead. By photographing the vessels on a revolving turntable, they have unrolled friezes telling tales in Maya ideology.

In these and other ways, archaeologists are trying to unravel the complex and little-understood symbolic world of the ancients.

# 10

# ARCHAEOLOGY TODAY AND TOMORROW

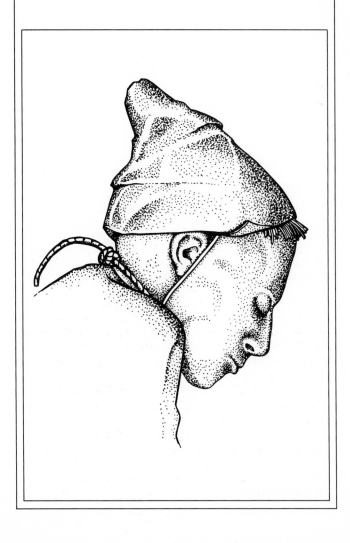

The nation's past is contained in the soil. That soil
is being distributed and redistributed at an ever increasing rate. Those of us alive today will be the last
ever to see any significant portion of it in an undisturbed state.

CHARLES MCGIMSEY, 1973

## MIDDLE-RANGE THEORY

Most archaeological research is based on the assumption
that because an artifact is used in a specific way today, it was
used in that way millennia before. Such studies of the relationship between past and present rest, however, on the
premise that this relationship has two parts:

The past is dead and knowable only through the present—
by archaeologists studying it.
Accurate knowledge of the past is essential to understanding
the present.
Archaeologists studying cultural change try to get the present
to serve the past by combining three interlocking approaches:
Ethnoarchaeology, the study of living societies,
Experimental archaeology—controlled modern experiments
with ancient technologies and material culture,
Middle-Range Theory—methods, theories, and ideas that
can be applied to any period and anywhere in the world

to explain what we have discovered, excavated, or analyzed from the past.

The expression "Middle-Range Theory" comes from sociology, and describes a body of theory that is being formed as archaeologists try to bridge the gap between what actually happened in the past, and the archaeological record of today. Lewis Binford writes that "the archaeological record is contemporary; it exists with me today and any observation I make about it is a contemporary observation." The present is dynamic, ever changing; the past is static, its dynamic elements long gone. Binford and others have been searching for "Rosetta stones" that permit one to use observations of the static past to make statements about its long-vanished dynamics. In other words, Middle-Range Theory will provide the conceptual tools for explaining artifact patternings and other material phenomena from the archaeological record.

By no means do all archaeologists agree that the archaeological record holds no direct information on human behavior. They argue that the relationship between human behavior and material culture in all times and places is what archaeology is all about. The controversy continues, but it is safe to say that ethnoarchaeology and experimental research, as well as analogy, have leading tasks in today's research into the past.

## THE LIVING PAST

We live in a world inhabited by an astonishing diversity of human societies. A century ago, many of them were still living in much the same way as their prehistoric ancestors. But the unchanging routine of planting and harvest, of life and death, of the seasons of game and vegetable foods, has withered in the face of Western exploration and technological superiority. Today, few of these societies are still enjoying their traditional lifeways. Many are extinct. The Tasmanians vanished within seventy years of white settlement; the Indians of Tierra del Fuego in the 1950s (Figure 10.1). Ishi, the last California hunter-gatherer, managed to live in his home territory in the northern California foothills until 1911. He saw

FIGURE 10.1 A group of Fuegan Indians walking along the shore; these and many other hunter-gatherer peoples are now virtually extinct.

all his companions wiped out by white settlers. The surviving Indian peoples of the Amazon region are rapidly fading away in the face of large-scale commercial operations in their forest territories. Soon all traces of living prehistory will be gone forever.

Anthropology has traditionally worked with non-Western societies and with peoples who have had to make far-reaching adjustments to the twentieth century. It is no coincidence that anthropologists have followed these people as they adjusted. Now anthropologists study their medical and psychological adjustments as the urban poor. But the archaeologist studies human culture of the past. Since 1877, many of the societies once studied by anthropologists have, by their death or transformation, become part of the archaeological record. No longer living groups, they have left behind them assemblages of artifacts, hierarchies of sites, a settlement pattern to be traced by surviving finds in the ground. The traditional cultures of the remaining hunter-gatherer and peasant societies are vanishing rapidly before Western technology, plastics, chewing gum, and the transistor radio.

## COMPARISONS

Early anthropologists collected vast quantities of information on traditional material culture of diverse societies all over the world. This material gave archaeologists a chance to make comparisons between still-living peoples and prehistoric peoples who lived at a similar stage of technological development. Thus, it was argued, the San, Australian Aborigines, and other living hunter-gatherers who had no metals could be considered living representatives of prehistoric, stone-using hunter-gatherers. An archaeologist who dug a twenty-thousand-year-old campsite in an arctic environment would turn to the Eskimo of today for comparative material from modern times.

But this type of comparison was obviously simplistic. In the first place, human society did not necessarily pass through uniform stages of evolution (Chapter 1). Second, each society has its own distinctive adaptation to its environment, which helps shape all aspects of its culture in many ways. And that adaptation was probably very different twenty thousand years ago.

Archaeologists then began to make analogies with recent societies in new ways. They worked back from known, living peoples into earlier times. They began by digging sites of historically documented Indians, and studying their contents, making full use of historical records to interpret their finds. Thus, photographs of Northwest Coast Indian homes taken in 1890 would be compared with excavated home foundations from comparatively recent times, say A.D. 1500. If the features of both were the same, then it was reasonable to interpret the design of prehistoric houses from this model. The house would then be traced backward into prehistoric times in sites many centuries earlier than the historic settlements.

This method very simply stated, is the basis upon which archaeologists use ethnographic records to interpret prehistoric artifacts and sites. Considerable controversy surrounds such interpretations, for sophisticated research methods are needed if comparisons are to be made between modern artifact patternings and those found in prehistoric sites. For this reason many archaeologists are strongly interested in "living" archaeology.

## LIVING ARCHAEOLOGY

Much of the ethnographic material available to archaeologists was collected when anthropology was a much less sophisticated study than it is today. Very often ethnographers collected object after object or information on customs without recording detailed information on settlement layout or artifact patternings, the types of information that archaeologists now need so badly. One can hardly blame the pioneers, for they were out to record as much information about vanishing cultures as they could before it was too late. And subtle settlement details hardly seemed a high priority.

Today, many of the settlements the anthropologists studied have themselves become archaeological sites. They are now virtually indistinguishable from prehistoric sites with their middens and crumbled hut foundations. They offer a unique opportunity to study the processes by which abandoned settlements turn into archaeological sites. Understanding these processes makes archaeological interpretation in general much easier, and so some archaeologists have gone out in the field to study "living archaeology" for themselves. Anthropologist Richard Lee, who has spent many years studying !Kung San of southern Africa, took archaeologist John Yellen with him on one of his later expeditions. Yellen spent many months studying the ways in which the San butchered animals and also the fragmentary bones that resulted from butchery, cooking, and eating. (Figure 10.2). He drew plans of recently abandoned sites of known age, recorded the positions of houses, hearths, and occupation debris, and talked to people who had lived there, as a way of establishing precise population estimates and the social relationships of the inhabitants.

Yellen found that the San camps developed their layouts through conscious acts like building a shelter or a hearth as well as through such casual deeds as discarding animal bones and debris from toolmaking. There were communal areas that everyone used and private family areas gathered around hearths. Some activity areas, such as places where women cracked nuts in the heat of the day, were simply located under a convenient, shady tree. Yellen recorded that most food preparation took place in family areas. Most activities in San

FIGURE 10.2  Living archaeology. A !Kung San brush shelter and windbreak, recorded by an archaeologist (F. Van Noten) shortly after it was abandoned.

camps were related to individual families. Theoretically, therefore, one should be able to study the development of the family through time by studying changing artifact patternings. To do so in practice, of course, requires very comprehensive data and carefully formulated research designs.

Ethnography and archaeology can complement each other beautifully. When Richard Gould was looking for archaeological sites in the Australian western desert, he came across a few bands of nomadic aborigines. These local people not only guided him to archaeological sites but also told him who had lived here, giving details of the sacred traditions associated with the settlements and describing the activities that had taken place at each (Figure 10.3). At Puntutjarpa rockshelter, Gould excavated stone tools dating back from modern times to about 6,800 years ago. Many of them were indistinguishable from tools still used by the locals. The aborigines iden-

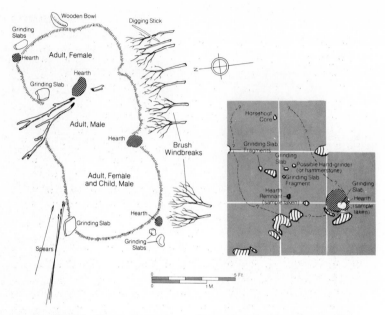

FIGURE 10.3 Comparison of a prehistoric campsite at Puntutjarpa rockshelter, Australia, at right, with a modern Australian aborigine campsite.

tified the tools for Gould, gave him their terminology, and explained how each was used. Gould then studied ancient and modern tools, looked at the wear on the working surfaces, and was even able to say that some five-thousand-year-old stone tools had been hafted with wooden handles. He could make this statement with certainty because identical modern examples were so hafted. Gould's research was successful because he combined archaeology and ethnography to study not only individual artifacts but also patternings of artifacts in ancient and modern sites. He even used his modern data to estimate a prehistoric population density for the area of 3.55 persons per camp.

Lewis Binford's study of the Nunamiut caribou hunters of Alaska was designed to learn as much as possible about an Eskimo group's hunting practices. The Nunamiut depended heavily on meat, supplementing their flesh diet with the par-

tially digested contents of caribou stomachs and about a cup-
ful of vegetable foods a year. They relied extensively on
stored food for eight and a half months a year, fresh meat
being freely available for only about two. Binford soon found
that Nunamiut food-procurement strategy was based on complicated decisions that involved not only the distribution of
food at different seasons, but the storage potential of different
animals, and parts of them, as well as the logistics of pro-
curement, carrying, and storing meat. Was it easier to move
people to the herds, or to carry meat back to base? His researches convinced him that the linkages between the facts
of animal anatomy and the realities of lifeway strategies held
the key to meaningful analysis of animal bones.

Binford studied the annual round of the Nunamiut, and
also their butchery and storage strategies, developing indexes
to measure utilization of different body parts. He also compared observations from modern kill sites to forty-two archaeologically known locations that dated to earlier times.
The Nunamiut research is valuable not only for the large body
of empirical data it generated, but also because it showed just
how locally confined any cultural adaptation is. The restric-
tion can, in turn, lead to major variations in archaeological
sites, as well as in artifacts and other archaeological remains
*even if the adaptive strategies and other factors affecting people's
decisions remain constant.* Thus, one can never assume that all
variability in the archaeological record is directly related to
cultural similarity and difference.

Living archaeology has the potential to produce valuable
results, especially for settlement studies. But it is urgent research. The few surviving hunter-gatherers and farmers still
enjoying their traditional culture are under constant threat of
extinction. Within a few generations, priceless information
will be lost forever.

## EXPERIMENTAL ARCHAEOLOGY

Archaeologists love experimenting with the past and have
done so ever since the eighteenth century. One ardent early
experimenter, a Dr. Robert Ball of Dublin, Ireland, blew a
prehistoric horn so hard that he produced a sound like a bel-

lowing bull. Unfortunately, his heroic effort caused him to burst a blood vessel and die. Not all experimental archaeology is so risky, however. Archaeologists have been making stone implements, floating over oceans on rafts, and trying to re-create the past ever since. Some of their achievements are remarkable.

Louis Leakey not only dug prehistoric campsites, but also spent many years perfecting his skills as a stone toolmaker. He could shape a perfect prehistoric handaxe and skin and antelope with it in a few minutes—a favorite demonstration at a conference. One of the most remarkable experiments of all was Norwegian Thor Heyerdahl's *Kon-Tiki* expedition, on which he attempted to prove that Polynesia had been settled by adventurous Peruvians who had sailed balsa rafts across thousands of miles of ocean. Heyerdahl did succeed in reaching Polynesia. His expedition merely proved, however, that long ocean voyages in *Kon-Tiki* rafts were possible. He did not prove that the Peruvians settled Polynesia.

People have cleared thick Danish woodland with stone axes and grown prehistoric crops in the American Southwest un-der conditions identical to those of centuries ago. The latter experiments lasted seventeen years. Good crop yields were obtained in all but two years, when drought killed the young crops. Experiments in living the prehistoric life-style have proved popular, especially in Britain and Denmark, where television networks have financed long-term experiments in-volving volunteer "prehistoric peoples." Controlled burnings of some faithful reconstructions of ancient houses have been undertaken, too, to show what the structures would look like when reduced to ashes—as structures are in many actual sites. British archaeologists have even built an entire experi-mental earthwork that they are digging up at regular intervals over 128 years. The resulting information on soil decay and artifact preservation will be invaluable for interpreting equiv-alent prehistoric sites.

Many recent experimenters have concentrated on replicat-ing such phenomena as wear on the working edges of pre-historic stone tools. Lawrence Keeley and other researchers have examined stone artifacts such as Paleo-Indian points un-der high- and low-power microscopes. They are now able to distinguish between wear polishes associated with materials including wood, bone, and hide. This approach is now reliable enough to allow one to state whether a tool was used to slice wood, cut up vegetables, or strip meat from bones.

Sometimes, edge-wear studies can yield remarkable results, especially when combined with *retrofitting*, reassembling flakes with the parent core from which they were struck. David Cahen and Lawrence Keeley collaborated in a study of a 9,000-year-old Stone Age campsite at Meer in northern Belgium. By reassembling some of the stone flakes and cores, studying the wear patterns on tool working edges, and examining distribution of stone fragments throughout the site, they were able to show that two people, one of them left-handed, had made some tools then used to bore and grave fragments of bone.

Experimental archaeology is principally remembered for its spectacular tests, like *Kon-Tiki* or the blaring sound of Tutankhamun's trumpets, blown for the first time in 3,300 years. The amount of data that can be derived from controlled experiments is, however, limited. Many intangible variables affected the design and use of prehistoric artifacts. And, as the Meer research shows, very precise research designs and carefully controlled data are needed to take proper account of such intangibles.

## THE FUTURE OF THE PAST

Experimental and living archaeology bring us into intimate association with the present, with the archaeologist as anthropologist. No one confronted with the results of Gould's work in Australia or the many excavations on Indian pueblos in the Southwest can doubt the essential continuity between many of the world's recent societies and the long millennia of prehistoric times. Anthropology tells a story of human biological and cultural evolution that climaxes in urban civilization and the extraordinary diversity of the modern world. But the very emergence of civilization has hastened the evolution of new, much larger, global societies. Scores of societies are now linked by religious beliefs, political ideologies, or remarkable heights of technological achievement. Our own Western society, with its ability in instant communication and its capacity to feed more people than ever before, has reached out to the farthest corners of the world in search of new economic and spiritual domains to conquer. The results for many societies have been traumatic.

The Polynesians encountered the Western world in the eighteenth century. A hundred years later, they were a shadow of their previous selves, exploited and missionized almost to death. Millions of American Indians perished as the frontier of the United States pushed inexorably westward. Few bands of Australian aborigines retain even a part of their millennia-old culture. The alternatives for the members of these societies were extinction or assimilation into a culture where they were, at best, second-rate citizens. Only in the 1960s and 1970s have some of them been able to stand on their own feet again, as newly independent groups or nations trying to reestablish their identity in a much-changed world.

Nationalism can be seen as one of the major historical trends of recent decades. It is manifested in new nations and in ethnic minorities who have begun an ardent search for their own historical identity. Alex Haley's *Roots* rightly caused a sensation when it recounted how Haley found his ancestry in West Africa. For many people, such oral traditions were lost in the enormous adjustment their nonliterate societies have made in the past century. Thus, archaeology remains the primary source of historical data about the Australian aborigines, the Tahitians, the American Indians, and hundreds of other non-Western societies. If asked whether archaeology has any use, one need only to point to the huge gaps in world history that still await archaeologists' attention—if any sites are left to excavate.

The breathtaking pace of agricultural and industrial development in recent years has taken a massive toll of the past. Thousands of American Indian sites have been destroyed by flooding under hydroelectric dams, by deep plowing and strip mining, and by thousands of acres of urban development and freeway construction. Pot hunters, too, have taken their toll. We may be the last generation of Americans to see many undisturbed archaeological sites. Charles McGimsey of the University of Arkansas has estimated that few untouched sites remain in his state. Probably fewer than 5 percent undisturbed sites are left in Los Angeles County. Despite many newly passed antiquities laws in recent years, which mainly protect sites on federal land, the danger is real that archaeology in North America is doomed. The finite resource base of sites is being eroded with little thought for the history these priceless archives contain. It is genocide, not of the living, but of the dead.

The popular interest in archaeology still revels in ancient mysteries, the excitement of discovery—and buried treasure. Many people regard archaeology as a luxury with no relevance to the cultural history of humankind. It is a means for gratifying their urge to possess things. Projectile points, Maya pots, and bronze swords look good on a mantle shelf or in a museum display case. So great is the demand for such treasures that a flourishing antiquities market has grown up to satisfy our greedy urges. Archaeological sites have been destroyed for commercial ends ever since the eighteenth century. The early collections of the Metropolitan Museum of Art in New York and many other major museums were very often accumulated by purchase of looted objects handled by large-scale dealers in the past. Today's prices are astronomical. So much damage has been done that more and more museums and wealthy collectors are competing for fewer and fewer finds. Entire Inca cemeteries and Maya ceremonial centers have been decimated in search of salable objects. Many sites in the American Southwest had been ravaged beyond repair by the early years of this century.

Almost nothing can be, or has been, done about the illegal trade in antiquities. Unscrupulous collectors and museums do not care, the dealers do not care, and the treasure hunting supports whole villages of poor farmers in many countries. Worst of all, the public as a whole does not care. Unfortunately, the future of archaeology lies in everyone's hands, and many people destroy archaeological sites without realizing it or because they consider them useless (Figure 10.4).

## ARCHAEOLOGY AND YOU

How can you become involved in archaeology? Are there career prospects as an archaeologist? What can a lay person

FIGURE 10.4 Two possibilities for the future of the past. At the top, removal of the Abu Simbel temples was an international effort at rescue archaeology. Here, the face of Rameses II is lifted to the new location of the Great Temple. At the bottom, pot hunters at work do irreparable damage to a site. Compare this scene of devastation with the excavations illustrated in Chapter 6.

do to help save the past? There are many ways to become involved.

Hundreds of archaeologists work in the United States. Many teach in universities and colleges, some in high schools. Others head up archaeological departments of national, city, state, or local museums all over the country or direct state archaeological surveys. Archaeologists work for the National Park Service and other federal agencies. Others support themselves by part-time teaching or undertake contracts on federal projects or for companies seeking cultural resource management services.

The research interests of these archaeologists range from early Indian settlements on the plains to historical sites in New England, from theoretical models of early agriculture to computer simulation. One can find almost more specialties than archaeologists. And many of America's archaeologists work overseas—in Africa, Europe, Mesoamerica, Peru, and even farther afield. You can find someone who will teach you almost any type of archaeology you want, above or below ground, under the water, even in the air. Unfortunately, however, job opportunities are in short supply.

Most archaeological jobs, whether in a college, museum, or university, require a minimum of a master's degree, most often the doctorate as well. The doctorate is a research degree requiring comprehensive seminar, course, and field training in graduate school and then a period of intensive fieldwork that, when written up, forms the dissertation, which is submitted to a committee of examiners. The average doctoral program takes between four and seven years to complete. Once you have the degree, you still have to find a job as a faculty member or museum officer somewhere. And that, in these days of great numbers of Ph.D.s, is not easy.

The M.A. degree normally takes one or two years of graduate work and gives you broad, general training in the basic methods and theory of archaeology, as well as world prehistory, with some specialization in a local area or in cultural resource management. The degree is satisfied by courses and seminars. You may have to write a library thesis as well and obtain some digging experience. The M.A. does not give you as much access to research funds and opportunities as a Ph.D.. You can, however, do invaluable work in cultural resource management or local archaeology. Various universities and colleges do offer certification programs for people interested in contract, conservation archaeology, work for which no Ph.D. is required. Consult your professors about such opportunities.

Anyone who considers becoming a professional archaeologist must have a superior academic record with in-depth coverage of anthropology and archaeology. A grade point average of "A" is a minimal requirement for good graduate schools. Some field experience on a dig or survey is also necessary, as is strong and meaningful support from at least two qualified archaeologists able to write letters for you. As for attitude, strong motivation to become an archaeologist is a must, and, for the Ph.D., a specific research interest. An archaeologist who thrives on hard work and who can tolerate some discomfort, a mass of detail, and long hours of routine laboratory work, will be a happy one. And those interested in the field should also be able to face up to a very tight employment situation. An interest in teaching and a moral commitment not to collect artifacts for profit or personal gain are the remaining prerequisites in this formidable list. If the list sounds severe, remember that archaeologists of the next generation have the future of the past in their hands.

Let's say you do want to become an archaeologist. Which graduate school should you apply to? This choice depends on your specific interests, and you should choose your school accordingly. It is wise to apply to more than one department and to make sure first that your faculty advisers really support your application.

Many people want to gain digging experience whether they intend to go to graduate school or not. The best way to learn is to take a course in field methods, then volunteer to dig for a period on a summer excavation. Details of digs are normally posted on anthropology department bulletin boards or at local museums. Alternatively, take a general introductory course in archaeology, then go to a field school. Many university-sponsored field schools offer academic credit for your work. Such summer programs are well worth the time, for they combine lectures and seminars with actual digging and laboratory experience. And the camaraderie of such digs can be a memorable experience.

Some people venture farther afield and join an excavation overseas for some weeks. Cheap charter flights have made Europe readily accessible. By contacting such organizations as the Council for British Archaeology in London, it is possible to obtain details of excavations in progress where volunteers are needed. Bear in mind that very few digs, in this country or overseas, pay you to be an excavator. At the costly end of the spectrum are package travel tours that take students to such faraway places as Israel to dig and learn archaeology under close supervision. These tend to be expensive experiences, often of variable academic quality. But whatever type of dig you choose, an excavation experience is a good way of testing your commitment to archaeology.

An undergraduate degree in archaeology is insufficient qualification for a job in the subject. But good undergraduate training can give you a perspective on archaeology that will be with you for the rest of your life. There are many ways to enjoy archaeology as an interested lay person. You can join a local archaeological society, participate in excavations and volunteer museum programs, keep an eye on endangered sites in your community. The background in archaeology you take with you into later life will enable you to visit famous sites all over the world as an informed visitor, to enjoy the achievements of prehistoric peoples to the full. Above all, you can influence the ways in which other people think about, and behave toward, archaeological sites and accidental discoveries. And your contacts with former instructors and other professional archaeologists may help you prevent damage to important, undisturbed sites.

This book may be the only experience you have of archaeology. We hope it has given you some insight into how archaeologists reconstruct the prehistoric past. But how can you help save the past for future generations? How should responsible people live with the finite resources of prehistory? Here are some fundamental guidelines:

**Treat every archaeological site and artifact as a finite resource that can never be replaced once destroyed.**

**Report all archaeological discoveries to responsible archaeological authorities** (archaeological surveys, museums, university or college departments, government agencies.)

**Obey all laws relating to archaeological sites.**

**Never dig a site without proper training or supervision.**

**Never collect archaeological finds from any country for your private collection or for profit.** If you must collect, collect reproductions.

**Respect modern and prehistoric Indian burial grounds and sacred sites.** They have deep spiritual significance to their owners.

Is there a future for the past? Yes, if we want one. It is up to all of us.

# FURTHER READING

The technical literature of archaeology is immense; we can guide you to no more than a few key references on each of the major topics covered in this book. For more detailed information, consult one of the major summaries listed here or ask your instructor.

## General Summaries

Two major college texts provide a comprehensive background on the method and theory of prehistoric archaeology. This text is a much shortened version of my own *In the Beginning*, 6th ed. (Boston: Little, Brown, 1988). R. J. Sharer and Wendy Ashmore, *Archaeology: Discovering the Past* (Palo Alto: Mayfield, 1987) is an equivalent volume.

The major developments of world prehistory are described in my *People of the Earth*, 5th ed. (Boston: Little, Brown, 1986). Another excellent account is Robert Wenke, *Patterns in Prehistory*, 2nd ed. (New York: Oxford University Press, 1984). J. Gowlett, *Ascent to Civilization* (New York: Random House, 1985) is excellent for the Stone Age. *The Adventure of Archaeology* (Washington, D.C.: National Geographic Society, 1985) is a beautifully illustrated description of how archaeology began.

## Special Fields of Archaeology

Historical Archaeology: Ivor Nöel Hume, *Historical Archaeology* (New York: Alfred Knopf, 1968). Classical archaeology is summarized by Paul L. McKendrick, *The Greek Stones Speak* and *The Mute Stones Speak* (both New York: St. Martin's Press, 1962 and 1961). Underwater archaeology is covered by George Bass, *Archaeology Underwater* (New York: Praeger,

1966) and the same author's magnificent *A History of Seafaring Based on Underwater Archaeology* (London: Thames and Hudson, 1972). Keith Muckleroy, ed., *Archaeology under Water* (New York: McGraw-Hill, 1980) is informative and well illustrated.

## Atlases and Dictionaries of Archaeology

The best atlas for the general student is David and Ruth Whitehouse, *Archaeological Atlas of the World* (San Francisco: W. H. Freeman, 1975). A good dictionary: Warwick Bray and David Trump, *A Dictionary of Archaeology* (London: Penguin Press, 1970).

## Major Archaeological Journals

The dozens of international, national, and local archaeological journals, are designed mainly for specialists. Among those carrying popular articles on archaeology are *National Geographic, Natural History, Smithsonian,* and *Scientific American. Archaeology* is a superb magazine for enthusiasts, whereas *Antiquity* and *World Archaeology* carry articles of wide interest to serious archaeologists. American archaeologists rely heavily on *American Antiquity,* the journal of the Society for American Archaeology. *American Anthropologist* sometimes carries archaeological pieces, and Old World archaeologists publish in *Man, Nature,* and the *Proceedings of the Prehistoric Society.* The *Journal of Field Archaeology* is of high technical value.

## Chapter 1: Archaeology as Anthropology

James Deetz, *Invitation to Archaeology* (Garden City, N.Y.: Natural History Press, 1967), covers many of the points in this chapter. So too does Grahame Clark, *Archaeology and Society* (New York: Barnes and Noble, 1965)—an old account that has never been bettered. Rose Macaulay, *The Pleasure of Ruins* (London: Thames and Hudson, 1959) is a delight for tourists. Massimo Pallotino, *The Meaning of Archaeology* (New York: Abrams, 1968) is a thoughtful account of the issues raised in this chapter. A history of archaeology: Glyn Daniel, *A Short History of Archaeology* (London: Thames and Hudson, 1981). *The Adventure of Archaeology*, already mentioned, is a more popular account. For American archaeology: Gordon Willey and Jeremy Sabloff, *A History of American Archaeology*, 2nd ed. (San Francisco: W. H. Freeman, 1980).

## Chapter 2: Culture and the Archaeological Record

Few archaeologists have dared to write a summary of the controversial issues covered in this chapter. Gordon Willey and Philip Phillips, *Method and Theory in American Archaeology* (Chicago: University of Chicago Press, 1958) is fundamental. So also is V. Gordon Childe's insightful *Piecing Together the Past* (London: Routledge and Kegan Paul, 1956). Later developments in archaeology can be surveyed in Lewis Binford's *In Pursuit of the Past* (London, and New York: Thames and Hudson, 1983). See also P. J. Watson, Steven Le Blanc, and Charles Redman, *Archaeological Explanation* (New York: Columbia University Press, 1984). A magnificent assessment of contemporary American archaeology appears in David Meltzer, Don Fowler, and Jeremy Sabloff, eds., *American Archaeology Past and Future* (Washington, D.C.: Smithsonian Institution Press, 1986).

## Chapter 3: Time

No one has yet rivaled Sir Mortimer Wheeler's classic description of stratigraphy in his *Archaeology from the Earth* (Oxford: Clarendon Press, 1954). Dating techniques are mainly described in journal articles, but Stuart Fleming, *Dating in Archaeology* (London: St. Martin's Press, 1977) is informative. So too is R. E. Taylor and C. W. Ceram, eds., *Chronologies in New World Archaeology* (New York: Academic Press, 1978).

Karl Butzer, *Archaeology as Human Ecology* (Cambridge: Cambridge University Press, 1982) and Dov Nir, *Man: A Geomorphological Agent* (Boston: Reidel Publishing, 1983) are of fundamental importance; so also is Butzer's *Environment and Archaeology*, 2nd ed. (Chicago: Aldine, 1971).

## Chapter 4: Space

Once again, V. Gordon Childe, *Piecing Together the Past* (London: Routledge and Kegan Paul, 1956) is one of the few accounts. Kent V. Flannery, ed., *The Early Mesoamerican Village* (New York: Academic Press, 1976) covers some key concepts, but is better read in the context of Chapter 9. For the law of association, read John Rowe's paper: "Worsaae's Law and the Use of Grave Lots for Archaeological Dating," *American Antiquity* (1962), 28:2, 129–137. Much of the literature for this chapter is scattered in periodicals: consult an expert.

## Chapter 5: Preservation and Survey

There is no comprehensive treatment of preservation in archaeological sites. Here are some examples of outstanding sites: John Romer, *The Valley of Kings* (New York: William Morrow, 1981) is fascinating on Ancient Egyptian tombs, including Tutankhamun. The Koster site in Illinois: Stuart Streuver and Gail Houart, *Koster* (New York: Anchor Doubleday, 1980). P. V. Glob, *The Bog People* (London: Faber and Faber, 1969) describes a number of well-preserved prehistoric corpses from waterlogged Danish bogs; even the skin and intestines survive. Sergei I. Rudenko, *Frozen Tombs of Siberia: the Pazyryk Burials of Iron Age Horsemen* (Berkeley: University of California Press, 1970), as translated by M. W. Thompson, examines spectacular prehistoric graves where the permafrost soil has literally refrigerated such organic materials as rugs. The remarkable Ozette site is described by Ruth Kirk, with Richard Daugherty in *Hunters of the Whale* (New York: Morrow, 1975).

Archaeological survey is a hotly debated subject at the moment, but mainly in specialist journals. You can get some useful leads by consulting either of the major textbooks referred to above. Cultural Resource Management is another difficult subject, remarkable for the complexity of its jargon. Charles McGimsey, *Public Archaeology* (New York: Seminar Press, 1972) is a pioneer work. George Gumerman's *A View from Black Mesa: The Changing Face of Archaeology* (Tucson: University of Arizona Press, 1984) gives the general reader a good impression of rapid changes in CRM approaches. George

Gumerman and Michael Schiffer, eds. *Conservation Archaeology* (New York: Academic Press, 1978) has useful material.

## Chapter 6: Excavation

The most widely available manual of excavation methods is T. Hester, J. Shafer, and R. F. Heizer, *A Guide to Archaeological Field Methods*, 5th ed. (Palo Alto: Mayfield, 1987). Mortimer Wheeler, *Archaeology from the Earth* (Oxford: Clarendon Press, 1954) is an immortal account of the principles, based on large sites. Phillip Barker, *The Techniques of Archaeological Excavation* (London: Batsford, 1983) and Martha Joukowsky, *A Complete Manual of Field Archaeology* (Englewood Cliffs, N.J.: Prentice-Hall, 1981) are basic sources for the serious student. For sampling: John A. Mueller, ed., *Sampling in Archaeology* (Tucson: University of Arizona Press, 1974). An exemplary case study of archaeological excavation in an urban setting is Kathleen Deagan, *Spanish St. Augustine: The Archaeology of a Colonial Creole Community* (New York: Academic Press, 1983).

## Chapter 7: Ordering the Past

V. Gordon Childe, *Piecing Together the Past* (London: Routledge and Kegan Paul, 1956) is still one of the best accounts of the problems of ordering. So too is Gordon Willey and Philip Phillips, *Method and Theory in American Archaeology* (Chicago: University of Chicago Press, 1958), which describes some of the archaeological units used in the New World. Robert Dunnell's *Systematics in Prehistory* (New York: Free Press, 1970) is a technical but fascinating account of classification problems. The concept of type is covered in this book, and the article by Albert Spaulding referred to by the director is "Statistical Techniques for the Study of Artifact Types," *American Antiquity*, 18:4 (1953), 305–313. Robert Whallon and James A. Brown, eds., *Essays on Archaeological Typology* (Kampsville, Ill.: Center for American Archaeology, 1982) updates the earlier literature and is a fundamental source. About the best summary of the ideas behind cultural process is Lewis Binford's *In Pursuit of the Past* (London: Thames and Hudson, 1983). Also, P. J. Watson, Steven A. Le Blanc, and C. L. Redman, *Archaeological Explanation* (New York: Columbia University Press, 1984) and Guy Gibbon's *Anthropological Archaeology* (New York: Columbia University Press, 1984). An excellent assessment of the present state of archaeological theory appears in *American Archaeology Past and Future*, referred to above.

## Chapter 8: Subsistence

Zooarchaeology is well covered by several books with a "how-to" emphasis, among them R. E. Chaplin's *The Study of Animal Bones from Archaeological Sites* (New York: Academic Press, 1971). Richard Klein and Kathryn Cruz-Uribe, *The Analysis of Animal Bones from Archaeological Sites* (Chicago: University of Chicago Press, 1984) and Donald Grayson, *Quantitative Zooarchaeology* (New York: Academic Press, 1984) are more advanced essays. Lewis Binford's widely read and controversial *Bones* (New York: Academic Press, 1981) is an essay about the basic problems of animal bones in archaeological sites. For plants: Jane Renfrew, *Palaeoethnobotany* (London: Methuen, 1973). The Tehuacán discoveries are summarized by Richard MacNeish, *The Prehistory of the Tehuacán Valley*, vol. 1 (Austin: University of Texas Press, 1967), whereas Frank Hole, Kent V. Flannery, and A. J. Neely, *Prehistory and Human Ecology of the Deh Luran Plain* (Ann Arbor: Museum of Anthropology, University of Michigan, 1969) describe the Deh Luran finds. Richard Ford's essay "Paleoethnobotany in American Archaeology," in *Advances in Archaeological Method and Theory*, (1979) 2: 286–336, is an excellent introduction, which can be amplified with Bruce Smith's "The Archaeology of the Southeastern United States," *Advances in World Archaeology*, (1986) 5: 1–92, in which Smith discusses some of the results gained from subsistence studies in an area of North America.

## Chapter 9: Interaction

K. C. Chang, *Settlement Archaeology* (Palo Alto: National Press, 1968) is a basic source, and Kent V. Flannery, ed., *The Early Mesoamerican Village* (New York: Academic Press, 1976) is essential reading for everyone interested in this subject, if only for the fascinating and hypothetical dialogues that communicate different viewpoints about contemporary archaeology. Teotihuacán: René Millon and others, *Urbanization at Teotihuacán, Mexico,* vol. 1 (Austin: University of Texas Press, 1973). A superb monograph on settlement archaeology: W. T. Sanders, Jeffrey R. Parsons, and Robert S. Santley, *The Basin of Mexico: Ecological Processes in the Evolution of a Civilization* (New York: Academic Press, 1979).

For social organization, see James Deetz, "The Dynamics of Stylistic Change in Arikara Ceramics," *Illinois Studies in Archaeology,* no. 4 (1965). Essays on burials appear in Robert Chapman and others, eds., *The Archaeology of Death* (Cambridge: Cambridge University Press, 1981). Jeremy A. Sabloff and Karl Lamberg-Karlovsky, eds., *Ancient Civilizations and Trade* (Albuquerque: University of New Mexico Press, 1975) and T. K. Earle and J. E. Ericson, eds., *Exchange Systems in Prehistory* (New York: Academic Press, 1977) are useful sources on early trade.

## Chapter 10: Archaeology Today and Tomorrow

Middle-range theory is best summarized by Lewis Binford, *In Pursuit of the Past* (London and New York: Thames and Hudson, 1983). His *Nunamiut Eskimo Ethnoarchaeology* (New York: Academic Press, 1977) is a detailed account of his own attempts to grapple with issues of Middle-range theory and ethnoarchaeology. For living archaeology, see Richard Gould, *Living Archaeology* (Cambridge: Cambridge University Press, 1980). The !Kung San: Richard B. Lee, *The !Kung San* (Cambridge: Cambridge University Press, 1979). This book provides background on all aspects of !Kung life-style referred to in these pages. John Coles, *Archaeology by Experiment* (London: Hutchinson University Press, 1973) is the best summary of this subject. Karl Meyer, *The Plundered Past* (New York: Atheneum Press, 1973) is required reading for all archaeologists and nonarchaeologists. Charles McGimsey, *Public Archaeology* (New York: Seminar Press, 1972) highlights the crisis in archaeology. Last, Ernestine Green, ed., *Ethics and Values in Archaeology* (New York: Free Press, 1984) assembles essays on these vital topics.

# SITES MENTIONED
# IN THE TEXT

These brief descriptions are designed to give a small amount of background on sites mentioned in the text. They are not meant to be precise definitions. Ask your instructor for more information and references if you need them.

*Acheulian.* A widespread early Stone Age culture named after the town of St. Acheul in northern France. The Acheulian flourished in Africa, western Europe, and southern Asia from before a million years ago until less than 100,000. The Acheulians made many types of stone artifacts, including multipurpose butchering hand axes and cleaving tools.

*Adena.* A distinctive burial cult and village culture in the Ohio Valley of the Midwest. It flourished between about 700 B.C. and A.D. 200 and was remarkable for its long-distance trading and distinctive burial cults expressed in large earthworks and mounds.

*Áin Ghazal.* An early farming village in the Jordan Valley, occupied some 8,000 years ago. It is remarkable for its clay female figurines, perhaps evidence for an early fertility cult.

*Ali Kosh.* Early farming site on the Deh Luran plain in Iran, where evidence for cereal cultivation was found by flotation techniques. The site dates to as early as 7500 B.C.

*Apple Creek, Illinois.* An Archaic site, where people engaged in intensive collecting of wild vegetable foods after 3000 B.C. They concentrated on hickory nuts, acorns, and other common species.

*Colonial Williamsburg.* Reconstruction of Virginia's first capital city, carried out partly with the aid of archaeological research.

*Giza.* The Pyramids at Giza were built in the desert near

Cairo during Egypt's Old Kingdom, c. 2600 B.C The Great Pyramid is 481 feet high and covers 13.1 acres.

*Hadar.* A region of Ethiopia where early hominid fossils have been found, dating to as early as 4 million years ago.

*Hohokam.* A southwestern cultural tradition that originated as early as 300 B.C. and lasted until A.D. 1500. The Hohokam people were farmers who occupied much of what is now Arizona. Their cultural heirs are the Pima and Papago Indians of today.

*Hopewell.* Between 200 B.C. and A.D. 600, the "Hopewell Interaction Sphere" flourished in the Midwest. Hopewell religious cults and distinctive burial customs were associated with an art tradition that spread far and wide through long-distance trading connections.

*Ipiutak.* A sea mammal hunting tradition that was a variant of the Norton tradition of Alaska in the first millennium A.D. Ipiutak sites are remarkable for their decorated harpoon heads and other art objects, especially in the permanent settlements near Point Hope.

*Koobi Fora.* A location on the eastern shores of Lake Turkana in northern Kenya, where the earliest traces of human culture have been found, dating to more than 2 million years ago.

*Koster.* From before 7000 B.C. until less than 1,000 years ago, hunter-gatherers and later farmers settled at this location on the Illinois River to exploit the fertile river bottom. The site is unusual for its long stratigraphic sequence of Archaic and Woodland settlements and abundant food remains.

*Laetoli* in Tanzania yielded the earliest hominid footprints, potassium argon dated to more than 3.5 million years ago.

*Lovelock Cave, Nevada.* A desert site in the far West occupied as early as 7000 B.C. Located near permanent swamps, it has yielded minute details of prehistoric desert adaptations over a long period.

*Olmec.* One of the earliest lowland Mexican state-organized societies, Olmec culture flourished from c. 1500 to 500 B.C. Olmec people traded widely, had a distinctive art tradition that depicted humanlike jaguars and both natural and supernatural beings, and developed many of the religious traditions that were to sustain the Maya and other Mesoamerican civilizations such as Teotihuacán.

*Olsen-Chubbuck, Colorado.* An 8,000 year-old bison kill site on the North American plains that revealed many details of Paleo-Indian hunting and butchering techniques.

*Ozette, Washington.* A coastal settlement in Washington state occupied for at least 1,000 years by ancestors of the present-day Makah Indians. Ozette suffered disaster two centuries ago, when houses were buried by mud slides and preserved in perfect condition for archaeologists to investigate in the 1970s.

*Pazyryk.* Siberian burial mounds of prehistoric horsemen, where refrigerated soil conditions have preserved every detail of the dead, including skin tattoos. The Pazyryk mounds date to about 2,300 years ago.

*Pecos, New Mexico.* An Anasazi pueblo in the Southwest that was occupied for much of the past 2,000 years, and provided the first stratigraphic sequence for southwestern prehistory as a result of A. V. Kidder's excavations.

*Shang Civilization.* Early Chinese civilization that flourished from as early as 2700 B.C., when the Xia dynasty arose in the north. The Shang dynasty rose to power c. 1766 B.C. and ruled until 1122 B.C. Its rulers occupied a series of capitals near the Yellow River, the most famous being Anyang, occupied c. 1400 B.C.

*Snaketown.* A Hohokam pueblo in Arizona, occupied c. 850 to 500 years ago, and famous for its ball court and platform mounds. The Snaketown people probably maintained trading contacts with Mexican communities to the south.

*Star Carr.* A postglacial hunting stand in northeast England dating to c. 8200 B.C., remarkable for the bone and wooden artifacts recovered from a small birchbark platform at the edge of a small lake.

*Stonehenge.* Stone circles in southern Britain that formed a sacred precinct as early as 2700 B.C. and remained in use until the second millennium B.C. Some authorities believe Stonehenge was an astronomical observatory, but this viewpoint is controversial.

*Sumerians.* Creators of the Sumerian civilization that flourished in southern Iraq between about 2900 and 2000 B.C. Sumerians lived in small city states that perennially quarreled with one another and depended on irrigation agriculture.

*Tehuacán Valley, Mexico.* A valley in which evidence for a gradual shift from hunting and gathering to deliberate cultivation of squashes and other minor crops, then maize, has been documented. Tehuacán was occupied as early as 10,000 B.C., with maize agriculture appearing c. 5000 B.C.

*Teotihuacán.* A vast pre-Columbian city in highland Mexico that flourished from as early as 200 B.C. until it declined c. A.D. 750. Teotihuacán maintained extensive political and trade contacts with lowland Mexico, and is famed for its enormous public buildings and pyramids.

*Tikal.* Classic Maya city in the Guatemalan lowlands, which reached its height in about A.D. 600.

*Ur-of-the-Chaldees.* Biblical city in southern Iraq that grew from a tiny farming hamlet founded as early as 4700 B.C. Known for its Early Dynastic Sumerian burials, where a ruler's entire retinue committed institutionalized suicide.

# CREDITS FOR ILLUSTRATIONS

Figure 1.1: Hirmer Fotoarchiv München; Figure 1.3: Colonial Williamsburg Foundation; Figure 1.5: Courtesy of Museum of New Mexico (Neg. No. 58337); Figure 1.6: Courtesy of Museum of the American Indian, Heye Foundation, N. Y.

Figure 2.1: Courtesy of the National Park Service; Figure 2.2: From *The Rise of Civilization* by Charles L. Redman. Copyright © 1978 W. H. Freeman and Company. Reprinted with permission; Figure 2.3: Adapted from Stuart Piggott, *Ancient Europe* (Chicago: Aldine Publishing Company, 1965); © Stuart Piggott, 1965. Used by permission of Aldine de Gruyter (A Division of Walter de Gruyter, Inc.) and Edinburgh University Press, publisher; Figure 2.4: Griffith Institute, Ashmolean Museum, Oxford; Figure 2.5: Carl Frank, Photo Researchers, Inc.

Figure 3.2: Illustration by Eric Engstrom from the book *Invitation to Archaeology* by James Deetz. Copyright © 1967 by James Deetz. Reprinted by permission of Doubleday & Company; Figure 3.3: Adapted from Richard MacNeish, *The Prehistory of the Tehuacan Valley*, vol. 3 (Austin: University of Texas Press, 1970); Figure 3.4c: From J. G. D. Clark, *Excavations at Star Carr*, London: Cambridge University Press, 1972. Copyright © Cambridge University Press. Reprinted by permission; Figure 3.6: Adapted from D. R. Brotherwell and Eric Higgs, *Science in Archaeology*, London: Thames and Hudson, Ltd.

Figure 4.3: Reproduced by courtesy of the Society of Antiquaries of London; Figure 4.5: Irven DeVore, Anthro-Photo.

Figure 5.1: Redrawn from "The Swanscombe Skull: A Survey of Research on a Pleistocene Site" (Occasional Paper no. 20, fig. 26.3) with the permission of the Royal Anthropological Institute of Great Britain and Ireland; Figure 5.2: Danish Information Office; Figure 5.3: Ruth Kirk and Richard D. Daugherty, *Hunters of the Whale* (New York: William Morrow & Company, 1974). Photo by Harvey Rice; Figure 5.4: University of Alaska Museum; Figure 5.5: Copyright reserved by Dr. J. K. St. Joseph.

Figure 6.2: Richard S. MacNeish and the Robert S. Peabody Foundation for Archaeology, Andover, Massachusetts; Figure 6.3: Courtesy of James A. Tuck, Memorial University of Newfoundland; Figure 6.5: From M. D. Leakey, *Oldavai Gorge*, vol.

III, "Excavations in Beds I and II," London: Cambridge University Press, 1971. Copyright © 1971. Reprinted by permission; Figure 6.5: M. D. Leakey, *Olduvai Gorge*, vol. III (London: Cambridge University Press, 1971); Figure 6.6: Peabody Museum, Harvard University; Figure 6.7: Reproduced by courtesy of the Society of Antiquaries of London; Figure 6.8: Wilfred Shawcross; Figure 6.9: Peabody Museum, Harvard University. Photograph by Ledyard Smith.

Figure 7.2: Courtesy of Lowie Museum of Anthropology, University of California, Berkeley; Figure 7.3: Illustration by Eric Engstrom from the book *Invitation to Archaeology* by James Deetz. Copyright © 1967 by James Deetz. Reprinted by permission of Doubleday & Company; Figure 7.4: "Nine-thousand-year-old Mesolithic artifacts," fig. 35, from J. C. D. Clark, *Excavations at Star Carr*, London: Cambridge University Press, 1954. Copyright © 1954. Reprinted by permission.

Figure 8.1: After Sonia Cole, *The Neolithic Revolution*, London 1959. By permission of the Trustees of the British Museum (Natural History); Figure 8.2b: Redrawn from M. L. Ryder, *Animal Bones in Archaeology* (Oxford: Blackwell Scientific Publications Ltd., 1969); Figure 8.3: From Richard G. Klein, *The Analysis of Animal Bones from Archaeological Sites*, Chicago: The University of Chicago Press, 1984, fig. 5.4; Figure 8.4: Cambridge University Museum of Archaeology and Anthropology; Figure 8.5: Patricia Vinnecombe; "A Fishing Scene from the Tsoelike River, South-Eastern Basutoland," *South African Archaeological Bulletin* 15:57, March 1960, p. 15.

Figure 9.1: From *Urbanization at Teotihuacán, Mexico*, vol. 1, part 1, © 1973 by René Millon, by permission of the author; Figure 9.2a: Redrawn from *The Early Mesoamerican Village*, edited by Kent V. Flannery (New York: Academic Press, 1976); Figure 9.4: Musée de l'Homme, Paris; Figure 9.5: Courtesy of Museum of the American Indian, Heye Foundation, N.Y.

Figure 10.1: Colonel Charles Wellington Furlong; Figure 10.2: Dr. F. L. Van Noten, Musée Royal de l'Afrique Centrale; Figure 10.3: Redrawn from Richard A. Gould, "The Archaeologist as Ethnographer," *World Archaeology*; Figure 10.4a: UNESCO, Paris; Figure 10.4b: Hester A. Davis, from "Is There a Future for the Past?" *Archaeology* 24:4, © 1971, Archaeological Institute of America.

# INDEX